Series/Number 07–154

SOCIAL NETWORK ANALYSIS
2nd Edition

David Knoke
University of Minnesota, Twin Cities

Song Yang
University of Arkansas

SAGE Publications
Los Angeles ▪ London ▪ New Delhi ▪ Singapore

For information:

Sage Publications, Inc.
2455 Teller Road
Thousand Oaks, California 91320
E-mail: order@sagepub.com

Sage Publications India Pvt. Ltd.
B 1/I 1 Mohan Cooperative Industrial Area
Mathura Road, New Delhi 110 044
India

Sage Publications Ltd.
1 Oliver's Yard
55 City Road
London EC1Y 1SP
United Kingdom

Sage Publications Asia-Pacific Pte. Ltd.
33 Pekin Street #02-01
Far East Square
Singapore 048763

Printed in the United States of America

Library of Congress Cataloging-in-Publication Data

Knoke, David.
Social network analysis / David Knoke, Song Yang. – 2nd ed.
    p. cm. – (Quantitative applications in the social sciences; 154)
    Rev. ed. of: Network analysis / David Knoke, James H. Kuklinski. c1982.
Includes bibliographical references and index.
ISBN 978-1-4129-2749-9 (pbk.)
    1. Social networks. I. Yang, Song. II. Knoke, David. Network analysis. III. Title.
HM741.K66 2008
302.4072′3–dc22

                        2007029680

This book is printed on acid-free paper.

     09 10 11   10 9 8 7 6 5 4 3 2

Acquisitions Editor:	Vicki Knight
Associate Editor:	Sean Connelly
Editorial Assistant:	Lauren Habib
Production Editor:	Karen Wiley
Copy Editor:	Brenda Weight
Typesetter:	C&M Digitals (P) Ltd.
Proofreader:	A.J. Sobczak
Indexer:	Gloria Tierney
Marketing Manager:	Stephanie Adams

CONTENTS

Quantitative Applications in the Social Sciences

A SAGE PUBLICATIONS SERIES

Quantitative Applications in the Social Sciences

A SAGE PUBLICATIONS SERIES

SERIES EDITOR'S INTRODUCTION

Social network analysis has been a bona fide interdisciplinary/ multidisciplinary method from the very beginning. Unlike some other methods such as multidimensional scaling, which has a unidisciplinary origin, network analysis can be traced to at least three disciplines: psychology, anthropology, and sociology. In psychology, psychotherapist Jacob Moreno, the founder of the journal *Sociometry* in 1937, developed the namesake method for measuring social relations to better study the relationship between social structures and psychological well-being. Anthropologist W. Lloyd Warner and psychologist Elton Mayo were responsible for the famed study of the Hawthorne Plant of the Western Electric Company in Chicago that led to Roethlisberger and Dickson's publication in 1939 of the by now well-analyzed bank wiring room data. The data are better known for the sociological reanalysis by George Homans in 1950 and by Ronald Breiger and associates in 1975. Other important contributions were made in the 1960s and 1970s by sociologists, including Harrison White and Mark Granovetter, that furthered our understanding of social networks and bettered social network analysis as a method.

A quarter century has passed since the series published in 1982 the first edition of this book, then titled *Network Analysis* by David Knoke, a key contributor to the network literature, and James Kuklinski. Since then, social network analysis has made huge strides forward and has impacted many areas of the social sciences. *Social Networks: An International Journal of Structural Analysis* was started by Linton Freeman in 1979 and has become the flagship journal for the discipline of social network analysis. Many national and international-level social surveys routinely include a social network component, either once or repeatedly. For example, the 1985 General Social Survey in the United States collected network data that saw many social science publications. Social network data were gathered in all three waves of the National Longitudinal Study of Adolescent Health from 1994 to 2002, also in the United States. In the new millennium, European researchers conducted the First European Quality of Life Survey: Families, Work and Social Networks. In recent years, computer software for social network analysis has mushroomed, most of it freely available on the Internet. Over 50 computer programs exist for network researchers, from Agna, a program designed for social network analysis, sociometry, and sequential analysis, to ZO, Tom Snijders's collection of programs for analyzing 0/1 matrices.

Faced with all these developments in the past two decades and a half, the first edition is sorely out of date, and the challenge for an update would be tremendous. David Knoke and coauthor Song Yang gallantly took up the challenge and produced a completely revised version of the book, now titled *Social Network Analysis*. As with the first edition, the second edition begins from the basics and issues of data collection before introducing methods and models of network analysis. However, even just for the basics, the new edition has included important additions such as a discussion of three major underlying assumptions for network analysis. Needless to say, the current book reflects numerous recent developments, for example, by putting greater emphasis on graphs and by including more advanced methods such as the p* model. Network students and researchers will find the book a treasure chest with many a golden guide for their quest for meaning from social network data.

—Tim Futing Liao
Series Editor

CHAPTER 1
INTRODUCTION TO SOCIAL NETWORK ANALYSIS

Public and academic interest in social networks grew rapidly over the past generation. *Six Degrees of Separation*, John Guare's play and film, popularized the small-world idea of social psychologist Stanley Milgrom, in which everyone is linked to everybody else through a few highly connected intermediaries. Another pop-culture manifestation was the "Kevin Bacon Game," a trivial pursuit challenge for movie buffs to identify the number of links to the eponymous actor via the costars of his costars. The mushrooming appeal of online social networking among high school and college students, using Web sites such as MySpace and the Facebook, paralleled the proliferating advice by the business press to exploit networking opportunities for profit and career advancement (e.g., Cross, Liedtka, & Weiss, 2005).

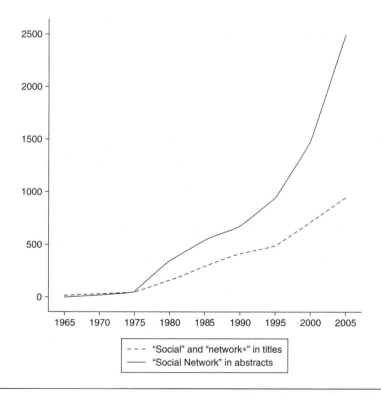

Figure 1.1   Growth of Social Network in Social Science Literature

SOURCES: 14 Social Science Indexes

As shown in Figure 1.1, social science publications with "social network" as a key concept accelerated exponentially during the past three decades, a trend showing no signs of slackening. A similar proliferation of network research applications to natural phenomena as well as to complex social systems occurred in mathematics and physics (Barabási, 2002; Newman, 2003; Watts, 2003). Network analysis became an institutionalized, transdisciplinary perspective whose basic concepts and measures are now widely familiar to researchers from such diverse fields as sociology, anthropology, economics, organization studies, business management, public health, information science, biology, complexity, and chaos theory.

Computer software that facilitates network analysis also mushroomed. General-purpose programs—such as UCINET, Pajek, NetMiner, STRUCTURE, MultiNet, and StOCNET—became widely available for routine network data analyses (for a detailed description, see Huisman & van Duijn, 2005). Numerous special-purpose programs also emerged to handle particular routines or problems such as identification of subgroups (Frank, 2003), study of hidden populations (Frank & Snijders, 1994), statistical testing (Tsuji, 1997), and computing optimal connection in valued graphs (Yang & Hexmoor, 2004). UCINET, with its continually updated versions (Borgatti, Everett, & Freeman, 2004), is probably the most popular and extensively used software package, providing comprehensive solutions and implementation of many network methods. It offers cascade modules of file input/output, data manipulation, network tools (MDS, clustering, and statistical analysis), and network methods (position, role, subgroup, blockmodel, and egocentric analysis). For these reasons, we use UCINET throughout this book to demonstrate network analyses on various artificial and empirical network examples.

This volume is a thorough revision of the first edition of *Network Analysis* by Knoke and Kuklinski (1982). In addition to providing a general overview of fundamental methodological topics, we cover new developments of the past quarter century. Space constraints mean that it cannot be as comprehensive as Wasserman and Faust (1994), but we examine more advanced materials than such elementary books as Degenne and Forse (1999) and Scott (2000). This book lays a concise foundation for the further study of advanced methods treated in greater depth by Carrington, Scott, and Wasserman (2005).

Our approach is didactic, aimed primarily at graduate students and professionals in many social science disciplines, including sociology, business management, anthropology, economics, public health, and human resources. College faculty could assign it as a text in graduate-level courses, use it for workshops at professional association meetings or summer instructional institutes, or study it as a way to learn about networks on their own. Graduate and advanced undergraduate students interested in social network analyses can read it to get a jump-start on their social network skills and intellectual aspirations. Professionals face many challenges in developing social network research, ranging from how to design a social network project, details and problems that may arise during network data collection, and alternative techniques for analyzing their social network data. Social network scholars may find this volume a useful brief refresher or reference book.

We frequently illustrate concepts and methods by referring to substantive social network research problems, citing examples from children's playgroups to organizations, communities, and international systems. We sought to write with a precision and freshness of presentation using concise language that minimizes technical complexities. The monograph consists of four parts. Chapter 2 introduces the ideas of relational data and networks, as applied to a variety of units of observation, levels of analysis, and types of measures. It contrasts relational contents and forms of relations, and distinguishes between egocentric and complete networks. The structural approach emphasizes the value of network analysis for uncovering deeper patterns beneath the surface of empirical interactions. Chapter 3 concerns issues in data collection: boundary specification, complete networks and network sampling, name generators and checklists, biases and reliability, relationship measurement for egocentric and complete networks, and missing data. In Chapter 4, we discuss basic methods of network analysis, including graphs and matrices; centrality, prestige, and power; cliques, cohesion, and connections; structural equivalence; visual displays, clustering, and multidimensional scaling; and blockmodels. Chapter 5 introduces more advanced methods of network analysis, including positions and roles; automorphic, isomorphic, and regular equivalence; logit models (p^*); affiliation networks; and the analysis of lattices. For readers who wish to analyze data as they read—an invaluable way to begin learning how to conduct network analyses—our example datasets and computer instructions are available in a downloadable zip file from links on the first author's homepage: http://www.soc.umn.edu/~knoke/.

CHAPTER 2
NETWORK FUNDAMENTALS

This chapter discusses fundamental concepts for understanding social network analysis methods. We use the terminology and definitions most widespread among academic researchers, but in instances of disagreement defer to sociological perspectives. We illustrate these basic concepts with citations to diverse research literatures, which interested readers should consult to deepen their understanding of how network analysis methods can be applied to investigate substantive problems.

To appreciate better the distinctive social network perspective of this book, a comparison to individualistic, variable-based approaches may be helpful. Many social sciences, possibly a large majority, assume that actors make decisions and act without regard to the behavior of other actors. Whether analyzed as utility-maximizing rational calculations, or as drive-reduction motivation based on causal antecedents, such explanations primarily take into account only the attributes of individuals while ignoring the broader interaction contexts within which social actors are embedded. In contrast, network analysis explicitly assumes that actors participate in social systems connecting them to other actors, whose relations comprise important influences on one another's behaviors. Central to the theoretical and methodological agenda of network analysis is identifying, measuring, and testing hypotheses about the structural forms and substantive contents of relations among actors. This distinctive structural-relational emphasis sets social network analysis apart from the individualistic, variable-centric traditions still dominating most social sciences today.

2.1. Underlying Assumptions

The network perspective emphasizes *structural relations* as its key orienting principle, where social structure consists of "regularities in the patterns of relations among concrete entities; it is *not* a harmony among abstract norms and values or a classification of concrete entities by their attributes" (White, Boorman, & Breiger, 1976, pp. 733–734). Entities may be individual natural persons, small groups, organizations, or even nation-states. The regular patterns of relations connecting a set of entities comprise macrosocial contexts, or overall structures, that influence their perceptions, beliefs, decisions, and actions. The central objectives of network analysis are to measure and represent these structural relations accurately, and to explain both why they occur and what are their consequences.

The importance of social network analysis rests on three underlying assumptions about patterned relations and their effects. First, structural relations are often more important for understanding observed behaviors than are such attributes as age, gender, values, and ideology. For example, explaining which elite families in 15th-century Florence supported the rival Medici or oligarchic political factions depended more on these ruling elites' economic, patronage, and marital relations than on their class and status attributes (Padgett & Ansell, 1993). Many attributes remain unaltered across the numerous social contexts in which entities participate (a person's gender, race, and education remain unchanged at home, at work, and at church). In contrast, particular structural relations exist only at specific time-and-place locales and either disappear or are suspended when participants are elsewhere (e.g., a student-teacher relation does not exist outside a school setting; a marital relation vanishes on the death or divorce of a spouse). A woman who holds a menial job requiring little initiative in an office may be the dynamic leader of her neighborhood association and an assertive PTA participant. Such behavioral differences are difficult to reconcile with unchanging gender, age, and status attributes, but comprehensible on recognizing that people's structural relations can vary markedly across social contexts. The structural-relational explanations favored by network analysts contrast sharply with numerous competing substantialist approaches that are premised on static "thing-concepts" as their primary units of analysis: essences, self-action, norm-based conformity, rational choice, variable-centric, and social identity approaches (Emirbayer, 1997). In conjecturing that patterned relations influence social entities apart from their attributes, network analysis claims to offer more comprehensive theoretical and empirical explanations of the sources of social action.

Second, social networks affect perceptions, beliefs, and actions through a variety of structural mechanisms that are socially constructed by relations among entities. Direct contacts and more intensive interactions dispose entities to better information, greater awareness, and higher susceptibility to influencing or being influenced by others. Indirect relations through intermediaries (in popular imagery, agents who broker connections for their clients) also bring exposure to new ideas and potential access to useful resources that may be acquired through transactions with others. For example, job seekers typically obtain less valuable information from their intimate circles, whose members already share and circulate the same intelligence, than from their weaker and more distant social contacts (Granovetter, 1973). Relational structures provide complex pathways for assisting or hindering flows of knowledge, gossip, and rumor through a population. Varied social structural configurations account for the diffusion of organic farming in Finland (Nyblom, Borgatti, Roslakka, & Salo, 2003) and the spread of sexually transmitted infections in American cities (Jolly, Muth, Wylie, & Potterat, 2001). Individual physical and mental health depend substantially on social support networks—whether anyone brings you chicken soup when you're feeling blue (Cohen et al., 1998). Structural relations are crucial to sustaining cohesion and solidarity within a group, but may also reinforce prejudices and fan conflicts with out-groups. Competitive and cooperative relations enable efficient implementation of planned organizational change inside a multinational corporation (Tenkasi & Chesmore, 2003), mobilization for collective action by social movements (Diani & McAdam, 2003), and operating "dark networks" for drug trafficking, immigrant smuggling, and terrorist campaigns (Raab & Milward, 2003). By channeling information and resources to particular structural locations, networks help to create interests and shared identities and to promote shared norms and values. Network analysts seek to uncover the set of theoretical mechanisms by which social relations affect social entities, and to identify the contingent conditions under which specific mechanisms operate in particular empirical contexts.

A third underlying assumption of network analysis is that structural relations should be viewed as dynamic processes. This principle recognizes that networks are not static structures, but are continually changing through interactions among their constituent people, groups, or organizations. In applying their knowledge about networks to leverage advantages, these entities also transform the relational structures within which they are embedded, both intentionally and unintentionally. For example, in Kenis and Knoke's (2002) theory of change in organizational field networks, antecedent communication structures affect subsequent strategic alliance choices. In turn, these interorganizational relations alter the flow of information, which creates further opportunities or constraints on future alliances. These dynamics exemplify the more general "micro-to-macro problem" in the theory of social action (Coleman, 1986). The core issue is how large-scale systemic transformations emerge out of the combined preferences and purposive actions of individuals. Because network analysis simultaneously encompasses both structures and entities, it provides conceptual and methodological tools for linking changes in microlevel choices to macrolevel structural alterations. Unfortunately, empirical network analyses of cross-level dynamic processes remain more a desired goal than a prevalent practice (Emirbayer, 1997, p. 305). But, as longitudinal network datasets continue to proliferate, new methods are emerging for conceptualizing and investigating network change (Faust & Skvoretz, 2002; Snijders, Steglich, Schweinberger, & Huisman, 2007).

2.2. Actors and Relations

The two indispensable elements of any social network are actors and relations. Their combination jointly constitutes a social network, as described in the next subsection. *Actors* may be individual natural persons or collectivities such as informal groups and formal organizations. Common examples of individual actors include children on a playground, high school students attending a prom, employees in a corporate work team, staff and residents of a nursing home, and terrorists operating in a covert cell. Collective actors might be firms competing in an industry, voluntary associations raising funds for charities, political parties holding seats in a parliament, or nations signing a military alliance. Sometimes network actors encompass mixed types, such as an organizational field comprising the suppliers, producers, customers, and governmental regulators of health care.

A *relation* is generally defined as a specific kind of contact, connection, or tie between a pair of actors, or *dyad*. Relations may be either *directed*, where one actor initiates and the second actor receives (e.g., advising), or *nondirected*, where mutuality occurs (e.g., conversing). A relation is not an attribute of one actor, but is a joint dyadic property that exists only so long as both actors maintain their association. An enormous variety of relations occur among individual and collective social actors that could be relevant to representing network structures and explaining their effects. At the interpersonal level, children befriend, play with, fight with, and confide in one another; employees work together, discuss, advise, trust, backstab, and betray. Among collectivities, corporations exchange goods and services, communicate, compete, sue, lobby, and collaborate. Which specific type of relation a network researcher should measure depends on the particular objectives of the research project. For example, an investigation of community networks will likely examine various neighboring activities, while a study of banking networks would look at financial transactions. Of course, some analyses scrutinize multiple types of relations, such as the political, social, and economic ties among corporate boards of directors. We present a general classification of relational contents in the next subsection.

Much social research continues to rely heavily on measuring and analyzing the attributes of actors as the units of analysis, whether through survey or experimental data collection. Although attributes and relations are conceptually distinct approaches to investigating social behavior, they should not be viewed as mutually exclusive options. Instead, many actor attributes can be reconceptualized as relations among dyads. Thus, a nation's annual volumes of exports and imports are characteristics of its economy. But the amount of goods and services exchanged between each national dyad represents the structure of trading networks in the global economy. A baseball team's aggregate won-lost record indicates its relative performance, but the ratios of victory to defeat for each pair of teams may reveal subtleties in a league's power structure. The number of friends indicates a child's popularity, but only analyses of all dyadic friendship choices can uncover important cliques and clusters. Relations reflect emergent dimensions of complex social systems that cannot be captured by simply summing or averaging its members' attributes. Structural relations can influence both individual

behaviors and systemic performances in ways not reducible to actor characteristics. For example, patterns and rates of the diffusion of technological
innovations are better explained by taking into account the structures of
communication and advice among actors than by their education, age, class,
gender, or race (Cowan & Jonard, 2004; Valente, 1995). Similarly, efforts
to combat epidemic outbreaks of infectious diseases like avian flu and HIV/
AIDS benefit more from knowledge about the structure of intimate contacts
than from assumptions about the susceptibility and resistance characteristics of a population (Jolly et al., 2001). The strong inference is that exclu-
sively focusing on actor attributes loses many important explanatory insights
provided by network perspectives on social behavior.

2.3. Networks

A *social network* is a structure composed of a set of actors, some of whose
members are connected by a set of one or more relations. These two fundamental components are common to most network definitions; for example:
"social structures can be represented as *networks*—as sets of *nodes* (or
social system members) and sets of *ties* depicting their interconnections"
(Wellman & Berkowitz, 1988, p. 4). Different types of relations identify
different networks, even where observations are restricted to the same set
of actors. Thus, the friendship network among a set of office employees
very likely differs from their advice-seeking network. Stipulating that connections exist among network actors does not require that all members have
direct links to all other actors; indeed, sometimes very few dyadic relations
occur. Rather, network analysis takes into account both present and absent
ties, and possibly also variation in the intensities or strengths of the relations. A configuration of empirical relations among concrete entities identifies a specific *network structure*, the pattern or form of that network.
Structures can vary dramatically in form, ranging from isolated structures
where no actors are connected, to saturated structures in which everyone is
directly interconnected. More typically, real networks exhibit intermediate
structures in which some actors have more extensive connections than
others. A core theoretical problem in network analysis is to explain the
occurrence of different structures and, at the actor level, to account for variation in linkages to other actors. The parallel empirical task in network
research is to detect and represent structures accurately using relational data.

The first researcher credited with using the term *social network* was
John A. Barnes (1954), an anthropologist who studied the connections
among people living in a Norwegian island parish. Barnes viewed social

interactions as a "set of points some of which are joined by lines" to form a "total network" of relations (Barnes, 1954, p. 43). The informal set of inter-personal relations composed a "partial network" within this totality. Barnes drew on the work of Jacob Moreno (1934), who pioneered hand-drawn sociograms of lines and labeled points for displaying children's likes and dislikes of classmates. Procedures for representing of networks visually as graphs and mathematically as matrices appear in Chapter 3. From anthropology and sociology, network ideas and methods spread over that past half century to many disciplines, which adapted them to prevailing theories and problems. For historical overviews of the origins and diffusion of network principles, see Freeman (2004), Scott (2000), and Knox, Savage, and Harvey (2006).

If network analysis were just a conceptual framework for describing how a set of actors is linked together, it would not have excited so much interest and effort among social researchers. But as an integrated set of theoretical concepts and analytic methods, *social network analysis* offers more than accurate representations. It proposes that, because network structures affect both the individual and systemic levels of analysis, network analysis can explain variation in structural relations and their consequences. J. Clyde Mitchell's (1969, p. 2) definition of social networks emphasized their impact on outcomes: "a specific set of linkages among a defined set of persons, with the additional property that the characteristics of these linkages as a whole may be used to interpret the social behavior of the persons involved." This perspective was echoed in the first edition of this book: "The structure of relations among actors and the location of individual actors in the network have important behavioral, perceptual, and attitudinal consequences for the individual units and for the system as a whole" (Knoke & Kuklinksi, 1982, p. 13). Similarly, Barry Wellman (1999, p. 94) wrote, "Social network analysts work at describing underlying patterns of social structure, explaining the impact of such patterns on behavior and attitudes."

2.4. Research Design Elements

Three elements of network research design shape the measurement and analysis strategies available to researchers: sampling units, relational form and content, and level of data analysis. Every network project must make explicit decisions about each element prior to beginning fieldwork. Varying combinations of these design elements generate the wide diversity of social network investigations appearing in the research literatures of many disciplines.

Sampling Units. The first steps in designing a network study are to choose the most relevant social setting and to decide which entities in that setting comprise the network actors. Ordered on a roughly increasing scale of size and complexity, a half-dozen basic units from which samples may be drawn include individuals, groups (both formal and informal), complex formal organizations, classes and strata, communities, and nation-states. Some two-stage research designs involve a higher-level system within which lower-level entities comprise the actors. Common examples of such nested social settings include corporations with employees, schools with pupils, municipal agencies with civil servants, and universities with colleges with departments with professors.

The earliest and still most prevalent network projects select small-scale social settings—classrooms, offices, factories, gangs, social clubs, schools, villages, artificially created laboratory groups—and treat their individual members as the actors whose relations comprise the networks for investigations. Recent examples include friendship patterns associated with classroom bullying and victimization among California adolescents (Mouttapa, Valente, & Gallaher, 2004), implementation of total quality programs in two metallurgy plants (Harrisson, Laplante, & St-Cyr, 2001), and community-based distribution of family planning methods in a Madagascar village (Stoebenau & Valente, 2003). Small settings have considerable advantages in sharply delineated membership boundaries, fully enumerated populations, and often access via permission from a top authority. However, nothing intrinsic to network analysis prevents applications of concepts and methods to larger-scale formations, many of which may have porous and fuzzy boundaries. Recent examples include adolescent romantic and sexual networks in a Midwestern city (Bearman, Moody, & Stovel, 2004), coauthorships of academic economists (Fafchamps, van der Leij, & Goyal, 2006), and strategic alliances among multinational corporations in the Global Information Sector (Knoke, in press).

Relational Form and Content. In addition to choosing an appropriate sampling unit, network researchers must decide on which specific relations to collect data. Relations among pairs of actors have both form and content, a dichotomy that Georg Simmel (1908) proposed in his analyses of association. Both elements are empirically inseparable and only analytically distinguishable. *Contents* are the interests, purposes, drives, or motives of individuals in an interaction, whereas *forms* are modes of interaction through which specific contents attain social reality. Simmel argued that the task of sociology is to identify a limited number of forms—sociability, superiority, subordination, competition, conflict, cooperation, solidarity—which occur across a wide range of concrete settings, social institutions, and historical contexts. A particular form can vary greatly in content. For example, the basic forms of superordination and subordination are ever present in government, military, business, religious, athletic, and cultural institutions. Conversely, diverse contents like economic interests and drives for power are manifested through forms of competition and cooperation.

The form-content dichotomy also applies to social network analysis. *Relational form* is a property of actor relations that exists independently of any specific contents. Two fundamental relational forms are (a) the intensity, frequency, or strength of interaction between pairs of actors; and (b) the direction of relations between both dyad members—null, asymmetric, or mutual choices. *Relational content* refers to its "substance as reason for occurring" (Burt, 1983, p. 36). This substantive content is an analytic construct created by a researcher that is intended to capture the meanings of a relation from the actors' subjective viewpoints. When people are asked, "please identify your close friends, friends, and acquaintances" in some social setting, the intended relational content is "friendship." The results of this query depend on how each actor first conceptualizes the meanings of the three proffered response categories, and then classifies the other actors according to recollections of diverse interpersonal interactions. Obviously, people may vary markedly in their interpretations of both the friendship labels and those activities that they consider to indicate greater or lesser intimacy.

The choice of relational content, also called *type of tie*, is largely determined by a project's theoretical concerns and research objectives. Thus, a study of health care networks could inquire into people's interpersonal sources of trusted information and advice about health-related matters, whereas a project on political networks might ask them to identify others with whom they discussed or participated in political affairs. Some substantive problems imply that more than one analytically distinct relational content should be investigated, in which case measuring and simultaneously analyzing two or more types of ties (i.e., *multiplex networks*) is an appropriate strategy. A comparative study of German, Japanese, and U.S. organizations engaged in lobbying the national government on labor policy legislation asked informants to report their separate policy information, political support, and resource exchange ties with one another (Knoke, Pappi, Broadbent, & Tsujinaka, 1996). We use some of those data in Chapter 4 to illustrate network analysis methods.

Although researchers' imaginative capacities to conceptualize and operationalize fine-grained distinctions among relational contents is virtually unlimited, in the spirit of Simmel, we offer a small typology of generic contents:

- *Transaction relations:* Actors exchange control over physical or symbolic media, for example, in gift giving or economic sales and purchases.
- *Communication relations:* Linkages between actors are channels through which messages may be transmitted.
- *Boundary penetration relations:* Ties consist of membership in two or more social formations, for example, corporation boards of directors with overlapping members.
- *Instrumental relations:* Actors contact one another in efforts to secure valuable goods, services, or information, such as a job, abortion, political advice, or recruitment to a social movement.
- *Sentiment relations:* Perhaps the most frequently investigated networks are actors expressing their feelings of affection, admiration, deference, loathing, or hostility toward one another.
- *Authority/power relations:* These types of ties, usually occurring in formal hierarchical organizations, indicate the rights and obligations of actors to issue and obey commands.
- *Kinship and descent relations:* These bonds of blood and marriage reflect relations among family roles.

Network analysts still have little sense of how various relational contents might be connected, because scant research has examined the structure of relational content domains. Ronald Burt's (1983) examination of how survey respondents perceived relational contents found substantial confusion, redundancy, and substitutability among the 33 questions posed to a sample of Northern Californians. He argued that just five key questions would suffice to recover the principal structure of relational contents in the friendship, acquaintance, work, kinship, and intimacy domains. However, we need much more research on the similarities and differences of meanings that people attach to commonly used relational terms and labels in a wide variety of network settings. A cognitive map of the structural connections among relational content domains would enable researchers efficiently and accurately to select specific contents that best fit their theoretical and substantive concerns.

Levels of Analysis. After choosing the sampling units and relational forms and contents, researchers have several alternative levels at which to analyze the structures in data that they collect for social network projects. Details of appropriate measures and methods appear in Chapters 3 and 4, but here we summarize four conceptually distinct levels of analysis on which investigators may decide to focus.

The simplest level is the *egocentric* network, consisting of one actor (*ego*) and all other actors (*alters*) with which ego has direct relations, as well as the direct relations among those alters. This set is also called ego's "first zone," in contrast to second and higher zones consisting of all the alters of ego's alters, and so forth. If a network's size is N actors, an ego-centric analysis would have N units of analysis. Each ego actor can, in turn, be described by the number, intensity, and other characteristics of its linkages with its set of alters, for example, the proportion of reciprocated relations or the density of ties among its alters. A recent egocentric study of crack addicts' personal risk networks found that users in Puerto Rico were more likely to engage in HIV-related sex risk behaviors with strangers or acquaintances than were New York addicts (Kang, Deren, Andia, Colon, & Robles, 2005). In some aspects, the egocentric level of analysis resembles typical attribute-based survey research, with a respondent's usual indivi-dual characteristics such as gender, age, and education supplemented by measures derived from that person's direct network relations. Egocentric network research designs are well suited to surveys of respondents who are unlikely to have any contact with one another. The 1985 General Social Survey of the adult U.S. population (Marsden, 1987) pioneered procedures for identifying and eliciting information about a respondent's alters, which we describe in more detail in Chapter 3.

The next level of analysis is the *dyadic network*, consisting of pairs of actors. If the order of a pair is irrelevant—as in marital status where both members of a dyad are either unmarried, cohabiting, married, separated, or divorced—a sample of N actors has $(N^2 - N)/2$ dyadic units of analysis. But if the direction of a relation matters, as in giving orders and taking advice, then the sample contains $(N^2 - N)$ ordered dyads. The most basic questions about a dyad are whether a specific tie exists between two actors, and, if so, what is the intensity, duration, or strength of that relation? A closely related issue is whether a dyad without a direct tie is nevertheless indirectly con-nected via ties to intermediaries (e.g., brokers, go-betweens). Typical analyses seek to explain variation in dyadic relations as a function of pair characteristics, for example, the homophily hypothesis that "birds of a feather flock together," or the complementarity hypothesis that "opposites attract." Contrary to conventional wisdom, an analysis of international con-flicts from 1951 to 1985 revealed that dyads linked by tight security and economic relations were only slightly less likely to engage in disputes than were pairs of nations lacking such ties (Benson, 2004).

The third level of network analysis is, not surprisingly, *triadic relations*. A set of N actors has $\binom{N}{3}$ triples, the number of ways to take N actors, three at a time. All possible combinations of present and absent choice relations among the actors in a triple generates a set of 16 distinct triad types. A basic descriptive question for empirical network analysis is the distribution of observed triads among the 16 types, a summary tabulation called the *triad census*. Substantive research on triadic structures concentrated on sentiment ties (liking, friendship, antagonism), with particular interest in balanced and transitive triadic relations (e.g., if A chooses B and B chooses C, does A tend to choose C?). Because we lack space to review triad analysis methods, interested readers should consult the research program of James Davis, Paul Holland, and Samuel Leinhardt (Davis, 1979) and a comprehensive treatment by Wasserman and Faust (1994, pp. 556–602) for details.

Beyond the three microlevels above, the *complete network* is the most important macro level of analysis. Researchers use the information about every relation among all N actors to represent and explain an entire network's structural relations. Typical concerns are the presence of distinct positions or social roles within the system that are jointly occupied by the network actors, and the pattern of ties within and among those positions. Although a complete network has N actors and $(N^2 - N)$ dyads (self-relations are generally ignored), these elements add up only to a single system. Examining hypotheses about the causes or consequences of structural variation at the complete network level of analysis may require several distinct systems, and be prohibitively costly. Nevertheless, analyses of complete networks are widespread. Some examples of complete network investigations are "friend" and "pal" relations among adolescent peers in Dublin, Ireland (Kirke, 1996), dominance hierarchies among the world's cities (Smith & Timberlake, 2002), and strategic alliances among firms in the Global Information Sector (Knoke, in press).

The four levels of network analysis imply that emergent phenomena at one level cannot be simply deduced from knowledge of the relations at other levels. For example, transitivity of choice relations is a substantively important variable for theories of friendship formation ("a friend of my friend is my friend"), which can be observed at the triadic level but not at the egocentric or dyadic level. As another illustration, consider two scientific research communities with roughly similar egocentric, dyadic, and triadic structures in their scientific discussion networks. But, if the first community's complete network is fragmented into several unconnected subgroupings, many scientists may be unable to communicate with others even indirectly. If the second community's complete network contains ties that bridge and broker relations among its subgroupings, we could anticipate a more rapid and widespread flow of information and higher rate of scientific innovation. This protean capacity of network analysis to address problems at multiple levels of analysis by encompassing emergent structural relations lies behind its rapid increase in popularity as a framework for theorizing and guiding empirical research.

CHAPTER 3
DATA COLLECTION

In any empirical network research, investigators must initially attend to three important issues before beginning to collect data: boundary specification, network sampling, and measurement of relations. Because setting the boundary around the set of actors to be included in a network project is an obvious starting point, we begin with this topic.

3.1. Boundary Specification

The question of boundary specification in network analysis can be simply asked: Where does a researcher set the limits when collecting data on social relations that, in reality, may have no obvious limits (Barnes, 1979, p. 414)? Laumann, Marsden, and Prensky (1983, p. 19) organized their initial answer around contrasting realist and nominalist strategies for specifying "the inclusion rules in defining the membership of actors in particular networks and in identifying the types of social relationships to be analyzed." Their subsequent typology replaced this strategic dichotomy with three generic approaches to identifying network boundaries: positional, relational, and event based (Laumann, Marsden, & Prensky, 1989). We examine both sets of procedures in this section.

Realist and Nominalist Strategies. In the *realist strategy* for boundary specification, a network analyst adopts the presumed subjective perceptions of system actors themselves, defining boundaries as the limits that are consciously experienced by all or most actors in the entity (e.g., a family, corporation, or social movement). Actors and their relations are included or excluded to the extent that the other actors judge them to be relevant. For example, Knoke and Laumann (1982, p. 256) applied this principle to select the core organizations of the U.S. energy and health national policy domains: "a policy domain is a subsystem identified by specifying a substantively defined criterion of mutual relevance or common orientation among a set of consequential actors concerned with formulating, advocating, and selecting courses of action (this is, policy options) that are intended to resolve the delimited substantive problems in questions." They excluded any organizations that domain informants did not perceive as influential in national energy and health policy making.

In the *nominalist strategy*, a researcher reaches network closure by imposing an a priori conceptual framework that serves an analytic or theoretical purpose for a particular project. In many instances, legal or other formal membership requirements draw clear boundaries, such as pupils in a classroom, lawyers in a state bar association, or organizations having general consultative status in the United Nations. As another nominalist example, consider that Marxist researchers identify boundaries of the working class as all employees having a common relation to a mode of production. The extent to which both the subjective-perception and analytic-imposition strategies produce coincident network boundaries is, of course, always an empirical question.

Positional Strategies. This approach uses the attributes of actors, their membership in a formal organization, or their occupancy of a well-defined position for inclusion in a network. Useem's (1979) study of American business elites exemplified the positional approach. Defining the elite to include persons who sat on the boards of the 797 largest U.S. corporations in 1969, Useem found a set of 8,623 directors. Knoke (2001) analyzed strategic alliances among corporations in the global information sector, identified by their presence on the Fortune 500, Fortune 1000, and Global 500 listings from 1989 to 1998. Feldman-Savelsberg, Ndonko, and Yang (2005) investigated collective memory choices among the members belonging to six Cameroon women's hometown associations in the city of Bamiléké, that is, women originating from the same village or chiefdom. Analysts who use a positional strategy may discover that an organization's membership list or roster is outdated, incomplete, or otherwise inaccurate. They may need to conduct their own census to compile a complete list of participants.

The positional approach commonly produces a set of actors occupying similar positions in a formal social structure, even when those actors lack direct relations with one another. Researchers should be acutely sensitive to how representative are network structures uncovered using positional criteria. Thus, the connections among business elites differ substantially from ties among lower-echelon employees. Strategic alliances formed between multinational corporations may be quite dissimilar from partnerships of small firms. Another issue emerging from networks bounded using the positional strategy is that the actors are often disconnected, comprising many small, densely connected positions lacking ties to one another. For example, the Cameroon women belonging to the same hometown association were often complete strangers (Feldman-Salvesberg, Ndonko, & Yang, 2005).

Network analysts using a positional approach should provide explicit justification for including or excluding particular positions (Laumann et al., 1983; Scott, 1991, p. 58). Researchers may apply nominalist criteria, setting an arbitrary threshold for their inclusion rules even where positions vary continuously. For example, to study large business firms, researchers might slice 50, 100, or 500 companies from the Fortune list. Where to draw a boundary may depend more on time and budget constraints than on some "natural" division between the included and excluded actors. Galaskiewicz's (1979) selection of organizations in the small city of Towertown vividly illustrates this process. First, he applied a territorial criterion that restricted the population to a geographic area. Then, an industry criterion excluded commercial establishments, transportation facilities, public utilities, real estate, block clubs, community organizations, and elementary schools due to his time and budget constraints.

Relational Strategies. This approach relies on knowledgeable informants or the network actors themselves to nominate additional actors for inclusion. Relational approaches embrace several procedures, including the reputational, snowball sampling, fixed list selection, expanding selection, and k-core methods. This subsection briefly describes the requirements and limitations of these relational strategies.

In the *reputational method*, researchers ask the most knowledgeable informants or experts to nominate a set of actors for their study. For example, investigators of two mental health agency networks first compiled master lists of community agencies (Morrissey, Tausig, & Lindsey, 1985). They then asked respondents to identify the five agencies from the list that were most important to them, or with whom they interacted most frequently. These two steps uncovered the sets of core agencies at two sites. Next, key informants, the directors of the Human Service Planning Council and the Rehabilitation Department, were asked to expand the core list by identifying additional important agencies from the master lists.

Reputational methods rely heavily on key informants to provide accurate and complete information, which raises concerns about the researcher's ability to locate informants capable of enumerating all significant network players (Scott, 1991, p. 59). Morrissey et al. (1985, p. 35) cautioned, "there are no standards by which the accuracy of this boundary-drawing [reputational method] criterion can be assessed. It is conceivable that different criteria could result in different actors being included and the subsequent analyses affected." Assessing the reliability and completeness of network enumeration using reputational methods is a formidable task. Often an assessment is possible only after a project is completed. Hence, network researchers should always justify their choice of key informants with strong theoretical and empirical reasons that are independent of the particular social relations under investigation (Scott, 1991, p. 59). But sometimes the problem of *sampling bias*—defined as a sample that is not representative of its target population due to not-at-random missing cases (Allison, 2001, pp. 78–81)—goes beyond the issue of identifying the right informants. Key informants, no matter how knowledgeable, always produce data systematically different from those collected through snowball sampling.

In *snowball sampling*, researchers begin with a small set of network actors, who are asked to nominate other participants with whom they have a specific kind of relation. These additional actors are likewise asked to nominate others, and the process continues until few or no additional names surface (Frank, 2005; Wasserman & Faust, 1994, p. 34). In its earlier, rigid version, each round of snowball sampling would generate the same number of actors (e.g., "name your three best friends"), and every actor at every stage was asked the identical questionnaire item (Goodman, 1961). More recently, these two conditions typically are relaxed to elicit differing numbers of nominated actors using different questionnaire items (Wasserman & Faust, 1994, p. 34). Because snowball sampling uses network actors' social relations to construct the sample, each round of nominations typically uncovers new participants who have relations with the extant actors. Thus, snowball sampling usually generates strongly connected social networks (Laumann et al., 1983) and is also called the *chain-referral method* (Heckathorn, 1997). A complex extension is *respondent-driven sampling*, which combines snowball methods with a mathematical model that weights the sample to compensate for its nonrandom collection (Salganik & Heckathorn, 2004).

Snowball sampling is particularly potent for finding members of a hard-to-reach population for social network analysis, such as drug dealers and users, illegal immigrants, sex partners of HIV-positive people, or underground militias. Due to the lack of a sampling frame for such hidden populations, standard survey sampling methods often yield insufficient numbers of cases. In contrast, snowball sampling starts by interviewing a small initial sample from, say, treatment centers or street sites frequented by drug users. The respondents are asked to provide locational information about other actors with whom they have the specified relationship. In turn, these nominees are contacted and asked to name additional participants. Because network data collection usually requires knowing the identities of egos' alters, obtaining informed consent, protecting anonymity, and assuring confidentiality raise several ethical concerns (Borgatti & Molina, 2005; Klovdahl, 2005). Human subjects committees may disapprove snowball sampling designs in which researchers recruit alters directly. As an alternative, respondent-driven sampling designs ask a set of "seed" egos to inform their alters about small rewards they may receive by volunteering to participate in the project.

In implementing network sampling, a procedural issue—whether to provide informants with a list of names or to allow respondents to generate their own nominees—distinguishes two selection methods: fixed list selection and expanding selection (Doreian & Woodard, 1992). In *fixed list selection*, a respondent is restricted to reporting ties involving a set of actors identified a priori by the researchers and their informants. In *expanding selection*, respondents identify as many actors as they wish without referring to a list of names. The implementation of expanding selection closely resembles snowball sampling procedures. In Doreian and Woodard's (1992) research on a set of child and adolescent service system program agencies, any agencies added to the network had to receive at least three citations from the extant directors or five nominations from the staff members. Agencies mentioned less often than those threshold frequencies were excluded. Doreian and Woodard reported that fixed list selection and expanding selection yielded drastically different networks on several dimensions, including numbers of actors, numbers of ties, density, and quality of ties. (Density was computed by dividing the number of observed dyadic ties by the total number of possible ties; tie quality was informants' assessments of the satisfaction, productivity, and worthiness of the ties.) Particularly, fixed list selection generated only 50 percent of the total actors, and 40 percent of the dyadic ties found using expanding selection procedures. The fixed list approach is more prone to nonrandom sampling bias; that is, it always produces a core set of actors and systematically excludes peripheral actors. This method yields an inferior result, a network without structural context. Unless conditions guarantee that both methods produce equivalent networks, fixed list selection, despite its low administrative cost, cannot be used as a surrogate for expanding selection.

The final relational strategy is the *k-core method*. Seidman (1983) proposed the k-core concept for finding subsets of actors within a large network, which typically contains many subgroups that are weakly connected to one another but densely connected within (Yang & Hexmoor, 2004). A subset is a k-core if every actor has ties with at least k other actors in the subgroup. By changing the value of k, a researcher can set more or less restrictive criteria for bounding a network. Doreian and Woodard (1994) applied expanding selection to demonstrate how the k-core concept could be used to define and locate network boundaries. (We discuss k-core methods in greater detail in Chapter 4.) By changing the k threshold, researchers can redraw the boundaries of a very large and sparsely connected network to make it either more restrictive (high k) or less restrictive (low k). For practical purposes, Doreian and Woodward (1994) recommended using a low value of k to establish the overall network boundary. A more inclusive network is less susceptible to selection bias, while analysts can always subsequently apply a higher k to create a more restrictive network. However, a more inclusive network imposes a greater data collection burden: Although a low k threshold produces a more inclusive network, researchers must interview large numbers of respondents at each nomination round, a costly and error-prone task. Lowering the k threshold also generates an exponential, rather than linear, increase in total number of network nodes. Although substantive applications of the k-core method are scarce, we believe it has great potential for empirically locating network boundaries. Recent network analysis software developments should facilitate k-core analysis.

Event-Based Strategies. This method draws network boundaries by including actors who participate in a defined set of activities occurring at specific times and places (Marsden, 2005; Scott, 1991, p. 60). For example, Freeman and Webster (1994) observed recreational users at a Southern California beach. They collected data on participation in 353 events involving 43 regular beachgoers, defined as persons who came to the beach at least three days during a month. An inclusion rule based on event participation starkly contrasts with the positional and relational approaches, which both ignore actor behaviors.

Because an event-based strategy relies on particular activities or events to locate a network's boundary, categorizing such actions appropriately is crucial. A daunting task for event-based analysts is to provide a sufficient rationale for selecting events that will answer a specific research inquiry. Researchers could include events that are either significant to a neutral observer or identified as important by knowledgeable participants. The event-based boundary method is vulnerable to having incomplete or missing data by overlooking some significant activities and actors. This problem is particularly acute for researchers relying on a single event to locate network boundaries, because many important players may fail to attend that particular event. Hence, observing multiple events would normally produce a more comprehensive network. Because each event involves a potentially unique subset of network actors, a multievent approach produces malleable boundaries: Every event yields a distinct network whose participants only partially overlap with those attending other events. Aggregating participants across all events should yield a more inclusive network which is better able to answer the research questions. For example, to study student interactions in a college dormitory, Freeman and Webster (1994) observed participants at events occurring in two visible settings, a cafeteria and dorm social meetings.

3.2. Data Collection Procedures

This section considers several generic data collection procedures for constructing network data, including single- and multiple-name generator methods, measurement of total personal networks, position and resource generators, and the use of archival documents.

Single- and Multiple-Name Generators. Name generators are mostly used in studies of egocentric networks where survey questionnaires collect information from each ego respondent about relationships among a set of alters with whom ego has direct contact (Marsden, 1987). Egocentric network researchers rely on two survey instruments: *name generators* that identify a respondent's alters, and *name interpreters* that obtain information on each alter and the relations among them and with ego (Marsden, 2005). First, an ego respondent is asked to name a certain number of persons with whom she or he has a specific type of relationship. Ego is also asked whether each pair of alters has the specified relationship. Finally, ego also provides information about each alter's characteristics, such as age, sex, race, and education.

Depending on a researcher's objective, egocentric network studies may use single- or multiple-name generators. A single-name generator relies on one questionnaire item to elicit the alters' names. The 1985 General Social Survey (GSS) module on Americans' core discussion groups vividly exemplifies the single-name generator design (Burt, 1985; Marsden, 1987). To elicit the alters in the GSS ego respondents' confidant networks, the interviewers asked:

> From time to time, most people discuss important matters with other people. Looking back over the last 6 months—who are the people with whom you discussed matters important to you? Just tell me their first names or initials.

Interviewers recorded as many as six names for each ego respondent, then asked, "Do you feel equally close to all these people? (IF NO): Which of these people do you feel especially close to? (PROBE: Anyone else?)" They next asked about ties among all pairs of alters:

> Please think about the relations between the people you just mentioned. Some of them may be total strangers in the sense that they wouldn't recognize each other if they bumped into each other on the street. Others may be especially close, as close or closer to each other as they are to you. First, think about NAME1 and NAME2. Are they total strangers? Are they especially close? (PROBE: As close or closer to each other as they are to you?)

Respondents were asked how long they had known each alter, how often they talked to each one on average, and various types of role relations (e.g., spouse, parent, child, neighbor, coworker, friend, advisor) in relation to the respondents. They also reported each person's gender, race, education, age, religion, and political party identification.

On average, the 1985 GSS respondents had only 2.94 persons with whom they discussed important matters, and 55 percent of these core discussion group members were kin (Marsden, 1987). The mean egocentric density measure of 0.61 indicated that a majority of alters knew one another. (Density of an egocentric network measured ego's perceived strength of relation for each pair of alters as $0 = total\ strangers$, $1 = very\ close$, and $0.5 = other$). American core discussion groups were more homogenous in age and education than the general population. Mean sex diversity of 0.68 suggested a balance of men and women in most core discussion networks. In contrast, the low racial/ethnic heterogeneity of 0.05 indicates that most alters had the same race, which Marsden (1987) attributed to the high level of kin nominations.

When the GSS name generator was replicated in the 2004 General Social Survey, a major change was a decrease in the mean network size, from 2.94 in 1985 to 2.08 in 2004 (McPherson, Smith-Lovin, & Brashears, 2006). In 1985, the modal respondent had three confidants, but the modal response two decades later was zero: almost 25 percent had no one with whom they discussed important matters. The greater decrease in nonkin ties led to networks centered more on spouses and parents, with fewer connections in voluntary associations and neighborhoods. Homogeneity among egos and alters continued to be very high, with educational heterogeneity decreasing and racial heterogeneity increasing. The analysts speculated about how changing U.S. demographics accounted for the rise in Americans' social isolation over time.

Ruan, Freeman, Dai, Pan, and Zhang (1997) replicated the GSS single-name generator in 1986 and 1993 surveys of Tianjin, China. On average, Tianjin respondents named more alters in their core discussion groups (4.58 and 3.30 persons in the two surveys) than the 1985 U.S. mean of 2.94 alters, and they were less likely to nominate kin. Compared to 1986, the 1993 Tianjin respondents named fewer coworkers, many fewer relatives, but more friends in their core discussion groups. These changes reflected macrostructural transformations since 1978, in which China increasingly replaced lifelong employment at one workplace with more flexible market-based employment. As the transformation progressed, people came to know more contacts outside their work spheres, which increased the chances of including such alters in core discussion networks (Ruan et al., 1997).

The 1985 GSS questionnaire did not provide cues about the content of the "discuss important matters" name generator, but left the burden of interpreting that phrase to respondents. This ambiguity triggered some concerns that the structure or composition of egocentric networks varies according to respondent interpretations of the phrase (Bailey & Marsden, 1999). For example, respondents who define important matters as personal and familial issues might be more likely to produce densely connected, kin-based egocentric networks than would respondents who define important matters as involving work or politics. To scrutinize respondents' cognitive processes in interpreting "discuss important matters," Bailey and Marsden (1999) used concurrent "think-aloud" probes with 50 interviewees, who were asked the standard name generator questions, followed immediately by some probes into their thought processes. Most respondents interpreted it as asking about personal matters, such as familial or interpersonal problems. Although preceding survey items apparently induced respondents to interpret "important matters" in alternative ways, these varying interpretations did not produce substantially different network compositions. Bailey and Marsden (1999) proposed four alternative strategies for future implementation of a single-name generator. The first strategy separates the definition of the content from the elicitation of alters: a respondent is first asked to define important matters in his or her own terms, then to name alters according to that definition. The second strategy involves exemplifying important matters, in which the researcher provides some examples that facilitate a respondent's definition of important matters. In the third strategy, the researcher explicitly specifies the meaning of important matters for every respondent. The fourth strategy involves rearranging the questionnaire sequence to attenuate any contextual impacts on respondent interpretations of the phrase.

Although a single-name generator produces a core set of alters, it elicits only a fraction of the contacts identified by using multiple-name generators. Researchers are often interested in diverse, routine activities beyond the core issue captured by a single-name generator. In an intriguing study of the concept "friend," Fischer (1982) reported that people use the term "friend" to describe quite different relationships. Instead of relying on a single-name generator, Fischer's multiple-name generators consisted of nine items such as house care; asking for a sizable loan; socializing; and discussing jobs, hobbies, and other personal matters. His survey of Northern California respondents elicited widely different numbers of alter names, ranging from 2 to 65, with a mean of 18.5 names per respondent. Moreover, respondents considered 11 of these contacts to be friends, evidently interpreting "friend" indiscriminately to encompass a broad spectrum of interpersonal relations. Two survey replications in Israel produce means of 14 and 11 names (Fischer & Shavit, 1995). Both surveys found that Israelis had higher-density egocentric networks than the Northern California survey.

To compare single- to multiple-name generators, Ruan (1998) administered 11 name generators to Tianjin respondents. In addition to the GSS important matters item, she included instrumental ties such as house care and money borrowing, and expressive relations such as socializing, confiding, and advice seeking. The GSS generator yielded a mean of 3.30 Tianjin alters, but the other ten generators together produced 8.17 alters. Moreover, the Chinese respondents interpreted "discuss important matters" as social expressive issues, with most respondents identifying the same set of persons with whom they socialized (going out to dinner, shopping, or visiting) as members of their discussion network. In contrast, persons nominated by instrumental name generators were least likely to be included in core discussion networks.

The largest egocentric networks can be produced by the "knowing" name generator, which asks respondents to report all persons known to them. Killworth, Johnsen, Bernard, Shelley, and McCarty (1990) showed that the knowing name generator could produce as many as 1,500 acquaintances in the United States and Mexico. However, to elicit a manageable list of persons with whom a respondent has significant contact, stringent limits are often imposed. Campbell and Lee (1991) summarized four types of constraints typically built into name generators: (1) *role/content constraint* restricts respondents to focus on only one or a few types of relations in nominating their contacts; (2) *geographical constraint* asks respondents to name only those persons residing within a specified area; (3) *temporal constraint* requires respondents to name their contacts within a certain retrospective period; and (4) *numerical constraint* limits respondents to naming only N persons who fit the name generator criteria (e.g., "your three best friends"). Most name generators use some combination of the four constraints. For example, Campbell and Lee (1991) presented 690 Nashville respondents with maps of their neighborhoods and asked them to list all neighbors in the nearest nine or ten houses whom they know by name. They next asked them to identify everyone with whom they had either chatted for at least 10 minutes or whose homes they had visited in the previous 6 months. Compared to several other name generators, the 1985 GSS "discuss important matters" name generator had the most restrictive content, numerical, and temporal limits, and elicited the smallest egocentric network size (mean of 3.01 alters) with the highest network density. Fischer's Northern California study, with its multiple-name generators, produced the largest networks (mean of 18.5 alters), but with lower density. The duration of the relations was the longest for the Nashville study, which did not impose spatial constraints, and contact frequency was the highest for the GSS. Campbell and Lee's (1991) study extended knowledge of how the restrictions imposed by name generators shape the configurations of resulting networks.

Positional Generators and Resource Generators. Social resources theory posits that social structures—defined by wealth, power, and status—are pyramidal and hierarchical formations in which social resources and access to these resources are embedded (Lin, 1982; Lin & Dumin, 1986). Although many studies have examined how the activation of social ties results in successful instrumental actions, until recently few researchers analyzed access to social resources. To solve the empirical problem of measuring actors' social resources, *positional generators* ask respondents to report whether they have contacts in certain social positions. To the extent that positions in a hierarchical occupational structure are reasonable indicators of social resources, investigating personal contacts with those positions divulges not only the types of social resources to which people have access, but also how they gain access.

How well positional generators capture access to a broad range of social resources hinges heavily on the choice of social positions. Lin and Dumin (1986) selected a list of 20 occupations with the greatest frequency in the 1970 U.S. Census Classified Index of Occupations. Those occupations spanned the upper and lower white- and blue-collar occupational divisions. Respondents reported whether any of their personal contacts, such as relatives and friends (strong ties) or acquaintances (weak ties), held each occupational position. Using a 1975 dataset containing positional generators to examine the job-seeking process, Lin and Dumin (1986) reported that the relationship between tie strength and access to prestigious occupations was contingent on a respondent's origin, as indicated by the father's occupation. When origin was high, strong ties and weak ties provided equal access to prestigious occupations. But, when origin was low, weak ties provided better access than strong ties to more prestigious occupations. Subsequently, Lin, Fu, and Hsung (2001) applied positional generators to study job prestige and income in Taiwan. They reported that Taiwanese society exhibited gender-based inequality in access to social capital. Social capital was more useful to men in obtaining prestigious occupations and higher incomes, whereas women relied more on human capital (education) to gain better jobs and pay.

Which occupations to include on the list, the most crucial decision in the research on positional generators, certainly depends on the research question. To study how cultural differences across social classes are related to social networks and relations, Erickson (1996) used positional generators derived from three major class dimensions: control of property, organization, and skill. Because her respondents all worked in the security industry, the 19 occupations based on control of skill reflected their security relevance (eight professional workers, four blue-collar workers, four policemen, two business managers, and one business owner). Interviewers instructed respondents, "Now I am going to ask you whether you know anyone in a certain line of work at all in the Toronto area, for example, whether you know any lawyers. Please count anyone you know well enough to talk to, even if you are not close to them." If respondents replied that they knew someone in an occupation, interviewers asked about the closeness of the relations, such as "just knowing," "knowing as a close friend," or "knowing as a relative." In a study of gendered social capital, Erickson (2004) purposely selected 15 male-dominated or female-dominated occupations, based on a Canadian census. Respondents were asked to identify whether they knew any men or women in each occupation. Erickson (2004) reported that men were more likely to know people in female-dominated occupations than women were to know people in male-dominated occupations. Moreover, because men were more strategically located in many social spheres, men's advantages in social networks were difficult to change, while both genders had more diverse ties to men than to women.

Positional generators produce egocentric networks measuring personal connections to several occupations in hierarchical ladders. To the extent that social resources are distributed within a pyramidal and hierarchical structure of occupations with differing status levels, positional generators accomplish the goal of capturing people's access to different occupations, hence to varying social resources. However, people often receive instrumental and expressive help from alters beyond those enumerated by positional generators that restrict selections to a handful of occupations. Researchers often broadly define individual social capital to encompass all forms of assistance that people may receive from their contacts. In particular, a resource generator typically captures individual social capital expressed as $SC = \sum_j S_j$, whereby j refers to resource items and S_j measures the availability of this type of resource (Van der Gaag & Snijders, 2004). Unlike positional generators that ask whether respondents have contacts with selected occupations, a resource generator asks whether people know anybody useful for specific resources. Van der Gaag and Snijders (2004) asked their Dutch respondents, "Do you know anybody who can..." help with a list of 35 items, ranging from "repair a bicycle" to "visit socially." They reported that 17 resource generator items formed four subscales that were internally homogeneous and weakly correlated. One subscale that measured access to incumbents of prestigious occupations correlated strongly with Lin and Dumin's (1986) positional generator. However, two subscales—access to information and access to instrumental support (e.g., help with house moving)—correlated only weakly with the positional generator, thus comprising distinct dimensions of social capital.

Measuring Total Personal Network. Some researchers are interested in measuring the *total personal network,* defined as all the alters known to ego, invented various name generators to accomplish this purpose. Depending on the particular procedures, total personal network sizes range from 250 to 5,000 alters (Freeman & Thompson, 1989; Killworth, Bernard, & McCarty, 1984).

In the *checklist method,* researchers first randomly select several names (either first or last names), and then interviewers read those names to randomly selected respondents, asking, "Do you know anybody with that name?" When a respondent recognizes a name, the interviewer asks name interpreter questions to elicit information about that alter. McCarty, Bernard, Killworth, Shelley, and Johnsen (1997) implemented this design by interviewing 793 Floridians with a list of 50 first names. Interviewers asked respondents to report any contacts having the same first name as those on the list. The respondents were told that they should know a contact by sight or name and have interacted within the last 2 years. Recording a maximum of 14 alters with this method, McCarty et al. (1997) found that the elicited alter sample underrepresented blacks, Hispanics, and Asians. However, they argued that this method is superior to other approaches in capturing a much more representative sample of the total personal network. The high correlation between the percentage of the respondents knowing alters with a given first name and the proportion of the U.S. population with that name suggested that its biases were not serious (McCarty et al., 1997, p. 311).

In the *reverse small-world method* (RSW), researchers first create fictitious targets, persons with invented names, randomly assigned locations, ages, sexes, hobbies, organizational memberships, occupations, and other socioeconomic characteristics. They then ask informants to identify all alters whom they believe could either directly deliver a message or be a link in a chain to the target. After eliciting the informant alters, researchers ask name interpreter questions about those alters' demographic characteristics, their relations with the informant, and the extent to which the alters know one another. Killworth et al. (1984) implemented an RSW method by interviewing 15 Jacksonville, Florida, informants about 100 American and 400 international targets. The informants named an average of 134 alters to reach these 500 fabricated targets. Most of the alters (86 percent) were friends of the informants, and more than half were male.

Freeman and Thompson (1989) concluded that RSW approaches capture only a portion of an individual's total network, because informants cannot name more alters than the number of targets. To address this concern, Killworth et al. (1990) combined the RSW with the checklist method and the

GSS name generator. They found that the mean size of total personal networks was 1,700 for Floridians and 600 for Mexico City residents. Drawing from the same dataset, Bernard et al. (1990) investigated the overlap among these different methods. They reported that the GSS name generator and the multiple social support name generator together accounted for only 18 percent of the total personal network generated by the RSW method. The checklist method (based on last-name matching) produced the largest personal network.

Archival Documents. Archival document data provide useful information for social network analysis, although the information was not originally collected for network studies. Compared with surveys, archival data are relatively inexpensive, pose no burden on informant time and efforts, and may contain high-quality longitudinal information when data are maintained over time. Archival data come in various forms, including Internet Web pages, personal letters, patent citations, book and article references, and computer network communications. Several online data providers—such as Lexis/Nexis, Free Edgar, SDC Platinum, and the U.S. Patent and Trademark Office—store large amounts of raw information about corporate boards of directors, strategic alliances, ownership of subsidiaries, and patent citations, greatly facilitating research on business organization networks.

New techniques to retrieve archival data are being invented all the time. With the Internet now a vast, rich repository of information about individuals, Adamic and Adar (2003) devised techniques to mine its interpersonal networks. Using customized software, they investigated the contents of the personal Web pages hosted on two university servers (Stanford and MIT). They paid particular attention to the texts, out-links, in-links, and mailing lists on each homepage. Their innovative attempt to mine Internet contents produced information not only on who knew whom, but also on the social settings in which these acquaintances occurred. For example, MIT students tended to know one another from fraternity and sorority affiliations, as five of the ten top-mentions of acquaintance social settings were fraternal or sororal names. In comparison, Stanford students were acquainted through more diverse social settings such as research groups, religious affiliations, ethnicity-based associations, and sororities and fraternities.

To the extent that personal letters and e-mails carry much information about interpersonal interactions, scrutinizing those messages provides fruitful data about personal networks, as well as social structures. This approach is particularly beneficial for historians whose subjects of ancient societies render survey methods impossible. For example, Alexander and Danowski (1990) investigated the social structure of ancient Rome through the letters of Cicero, the renowned orator and influential politician who straddled two elite social classes: the "knight class," which was without office-holding, and the "senatorial class" of officeholders. They reviewed 280 letters between Cicero and his acquaintances, friends, and relatives spanning 18 years. Their data management program recorded 1,914 relations among 524 individuals, including the name and rank of both persons, and such relational contents as giving, ordering, serving as intermediary, helping, describing in a negative way, and visiting. A major finding was that, although senators and knights opposed one another on particular issues, they appeared to make up a single, well-integrated, and interlocked social class.

Journal publications and patents, both with extensive citation lists, provide another good data source for social network analysts. Hargens (2000) studied the citation patterns of three physical sciences, three social sciences, and one humanity. For each discipline, Hargens first constructed a list of journal publications using citation index services and expert consultants. Then he recorded the references or footnotes in each paper that cited other papers, thus constructing complete networks for each area. Hargens found that researchers cited other work for various purposes, ranging from identifying with a general theoretical strand to correcting detailed computation procedures. In particular, physical science citations were mostly rejections or corrections of specific experimental methods, whereas social scientists mostly identified with or challenged the fundamental assumptions underlying the whole discipline. Disputes with previous work were much more common in literary criticism than in the physical and social sciences.

The patent process produces a rich data source for researchers interested in studying networks of knowledge flow. In their study of technological niches, Podolny and Stuart (1995) extensively analyzed patent citation lists. To receive patents, technology innovators file petitions with the U.S. Patent Office. As part of the application procedure, they must list previously issued patents serving as important building blocks. Patent examiners need to verify that a list includes all relevant antecedent inventions. Using a Lexis/ Nexis online database, Podolny and Stuart (1995) examined the U.S. semiconductor device patents granted to worldwide semiconductor inventors and manufacturers from 1976 to 1991. They measured technological niches as consisting of a set of innovations, linked by ties signifying knowledge flows from one innovation to another. Thus, each granted patent was a new focal innovation entering into a given technological niche. The patent citation list of a focal innovation provided information on its links to all prior building-block innovations and later patents citing that focal patent indicate its ties to subsequent innovations that build on the focal innovation. Thus, a technological niche comprises egocentric networks, consisting of a focal innovation and the ties linking it to other patented innovations.

Although investigating citation lists enables the construction of networks among academic authors or patents, two significant differences occur (Meyer, 2000). First, journal articles tend to cite a broad range of publications, whereas patent citations have a narrower scope, citing only those prior inventions contributing significantly to an innovation. Second, journal citations serve a broad array of purposes, such as giving credit to related work, correcting one's past work, and disputing previous claims (Meyer, 2000). In contrast, the more restrictive purpose of patent citation is to acknowledge previous works serving as the building blocks for the current invention. Thus, the networks constructed using patent and journal citations may differ fundamentally in their contents, necessitating careful distinctions among them.

Governmental and economic organizations have been assembling massive amounts of information about interactions among employees and also among powerful organizations. However, those valuable data sources are largely overlooked and scarcely tapped by organizational theorists (Perrow, 1986, pp. 172–173). One exception was Baker and Faulkner's (1993) study, which used the Kefauver Committee report—sworn testimony before the U.S. Senate Judiciary Subcommittee on Antitrust and Monopoly about corporate conspiracies. The authors uncovered the structure of illegal corporate communication networks and the factors driving them.

With the rapidly increasing application of computer network technologies since the 1990s, electronic communications are no longer restricted to a few technical experts, but increasingly involve the general public. New technologies are deployed to monitor or even stimulate communications between network users, allowing researchers to scrutinize communication flows to reveal interaction patterns. Social network researchers can obtain rich network data by examining such computer-mediated communication (CMC) systems as electronic mail, computer bulletin boards, voice messaging, and other "groupware" (Rice, 1990, 1994; Rice, Borgman, Bednarski, & Hart, 1989). Because a monitoring program generally stores all interactions within a CMC system, its network data comprise a census of all interactions among system users. However, for network analysts, scrutinizing every interaction can be overwhelming in computational time and cost. More cogently, as the communications vary greatly in content, time, and purpose, complete communication data may not be pertinent. CMC researchers can reduce their data loads by applying three types of inclusion rules: (1) In role-based studies, researchers screen either senders or recipients based on their roles, such as managers or accountants. (2) In time-based studies, researchers set a time frame within which to collect data on all the communications. (3) In content-based studies, researchers scan content or subject headers to select only messages fitting their research questions. Customized computer software can greatly facilitate content-based inclusion by conducting quick keyword searches of large network data repositories.

Compared to self-report questionnaire surveys, CMC analyses are less obtrusive and more immune from measurement errors. For example, when the self-reported relations of two individuals disagree, distinguishing such sources of measurement error as inaccurate recall, biased responses, and questionnaire wording becomes impossible (Rice, 1994, p. 176). However, computer-monitored network data accurately reflect the contents of the CMC messages, so hypotheses involving reciprocity can be explicitly separated and tested. Although CMC data are more accurate than self-report data, they are not necessarily more valid. They often represent different aspects of human communication (Rice et al., 1989). For example, e-mail communications probably reflect work-related activities more accurately than social activities among friends and family. As part of their agreement to use an e-mail system hosted on a workplace server, employees typically sign consent forms for voluntarily sharing their communications. Thus, depending on the topic, researchers should be cautious about data generated by CMC systems. Monitoring e-mail communications among users of a company's server may yield rich data about the network structure of work-related communication, but hardly any useful information on employees' after-hours affairs. Relying solely on CMC system may also miss some communication subtleties that turn out to be important. Much message content is insignificant and routine, yet a single sentence might be highly consequential. Thus, researchers should be sensitive to CMC data analyses that strip away valuable contextual cues, removing some underlying salience of communication events (Rice, 1994, p. 177).

Recent advances in CMC extensively use cyber infrastructure to facilitate social network analysis (Berman & Brady, 2005). Cyber infrastructure encompasses a broad range of cybertools such as high-performance computers and networks; personal electronic devices (instant messagers, Blackberry, and personal digital assistant); data acquisition, management, and analysis services; and visualization facilities. Cyber infrastructure presents enormous novel opportunities for social network analysts. For example, high-performance computer servers routinely record textual messages among users of the World Wide Web and personal electronic devices. Analyzing those messages yields important social interaction patterns and network configurations. Immense opportunities also come with tremendous challenges, from technical problems of how to acquire, store, and analyze voluminous data to sociolegal issues of how to ensure informed agreement and to protect privacy and confidentiality. Thus, cyber infrastructure–facilitated network analysis requires unprecedented collaboration across diverse disciplines, including social science, law, electronics, and computer science.

Recent work by Adamic and Adar (2003) exemplified how cybertools can acquire and analyze large volumes of information circulating in cyberspace to extend our understanding of certain substantive issues in social network analysis. To study small-world phenomena, they collected data from an e-mail network among employees of a Hewlett Packard lab and from a social networking Web page among more than 2,000 Stanford University students. The communication network contained 4,000 e-mails between 430 individuals who exchanged at least six e-mails during the 3-month observation. The Web page network data came from a community Web site, Club Nexus, which invited Stanford students to join the club and list their friends in their registration. The registration process also required registrants to report their majors, gender, personalities, dorm locations, and hobbies. Friends were asked to reciprocate the tie by registering with Club Nexus. Nonreciprocated ties were dropped from the database. To locate the targets of the communications, Adamic and Adar executed three search strategies on the observed e-mail network, each reflecting an underlying theoretical argument. The high degree–seeking strategy selected the individual who was likely to know a target by virtue of knowing many people. The second strategy involved passing a message to the contact person closest to the target in the organizational hierarchy. The third strategy passed a message to the contact geographically nearest the target. Simulating the three strategies on both networks, Adamic and Adar reported that the second strategy, positional search, found the shortest path between pairs in the lab network. However, none of the search strategies produced reasonably short distances in the club network.

3.3. Cognitive Social Structure

Although one of the most common questions about social networks may be, "Who knows whom?" perhaps the most relevant question for cognitive social structure (CSS) analysts is, "Who knows who knows whom?" Researchers use CSS data to investigate variations in informants' perceptions of network relations. Although informants could be external observers, usually they are also participants in the networks about which they report. To create a CSS dataset, a researcher asks each participant to report her or his subjective perceptions of every dyadic relation in the network; for example, using a complete list of all pairs of actors to check off the perceived presence of directed ties. For a network of N actors, a complete CSS dataset for one type of relationship consists of N *cognitive maps* showing the presence and absence of ties from every participant-informant's point of view. Given the potentially huge time and recall burdens—each informant must make $N^2 - N$ judgments about the specified directed dyadic relations—CSS data collection is often restricted either to very small networks or to a task with limited scope (e.g., "Who are X's three closest friends?"; "Which five persons does Y trust most?"). For example, Krackhardt (1987) collected CSS data on two types of relations—advice seeking and friendship—from 21 managerial employees, resulting in two sets of 21 cognitive maps each displaying $(21)^2 - 21 = 420$ directed ties. An egocentric network is a special case of CSS, where an informant describes only the perceived relations among her or his direct contacts, but not the ties to all other network members.

Two common uses of CSS datasets are (1) to determine the amount of consensus on network structures as perceived by the participants and (2) to assess biases in perceived network structures in comparison to some criterion. *Consensus* is the extent of agreement between two or more informants' judgments or assessments of social relations. An important theoretical issue is whether consensus is higher among actors who have similar attributes (such as race, gender, or age), or whether actors who share relational ties (or occupy similar network locations) are more likely to agree in their perceptions of the network. *Bias* refers to the accuracy of an informant's perceptions of network relations when compared to a specified criterion (see the following section for more about informant bias). One criterion is an aggregation of all the other participants' perceived networks. Another criterion is relational data obtained from direct observations of the participants' behaviors. Network analysts have long observed major discrepancies between self-reports and behavioral measures of interaction, and have proposed methods to handle such inconsistencies. Although the large majority of network data is collected using face-to-face or telephone interviews, most researchers seldom investigate the cognitive social structures that respondents or informants use to form their responses. Analysts typically treat all responses as unequivocally "objective" social facts. However, a few scholars have sought to understand and measure the sources of divergence between information based on respondent perceptions and behavioral observations (e.g., Batchelder, 2002; Carley & Krackhardt, 1996; Casciaro, 1998; Freeman, 1992; Johnson & Orbach, 2002; Koehly & Pattison, 2005; Krackhardt, 1987).

Cognitive social structure also helps researchers identify systematic perceptual errors in respondent self-reports. Kumbasar, Romney, and Batchelder (1994) constructed a cognitive social structure by interviewing 25 computer hardware engineers. Each informant was presented with a randomly selected engineer's name and asked to mark, on a list of all 25 engineers, which persons they perceived to be a friend of the selected engineer. This process was repeated for all names, including the informant's own name. The resulting 25 cognitive maps could then be aggregated across all the engineer-informants into a global network, using matrix algebra methods (see Chapter 4). Comparing the self-perceived friendship networks with the global network, Kumbasar et al. (1994) concluded that individuals tended to see themselves as closer to the center of their own network representations than to the global network center. In addition, individuals tend to construct a cognitively consistent network; that is, they viewed themselves as surrounded by friends, who also had numerous friendships among themselves.

The finding that informants tend to construct a cognitively consistent image is not novel. The rich literature on cognitive psychology has long argued that people experience psychological or emotional stress when they encounter unbalanced relations (Heider, 1958; Newcomb, 1961). Consequently, individuals seeing unbalanced relations tend to activate a "balance schema": they change their perceptions to achieve a balanced image of those relations. However, because this cognitive correction occurs primarily among friends, especially close friends, people seem relatively unaffected by perceived imbalances among persons with whom they are not friends. Indeed, when individuals are not directly connected, little discomfort results from any perceived imbalances. Thus, although in trying to maintain their psychological comfort, informants are more prone to providing distorted and biased information about their friends' relations, their reports about more distant contacts seem less susceptible to biases and distortions.

Contrary to this conventional wisdom, Krackhardt and Kilduff (1999), drawing from Taylor and Fiske's (1978) cognitive miser model, stated that informants typically have less knowledge about those distant relations with whom they are not directly linked. By activating the balance schema to fill in knowledge gaps, informants are biased in reporting both close and distant relations. But their motives differ: For close relations, the balanced schema is activated to achieve psychological and emotional comfort, but for distant relations, the schema compensates for the lack of knowledge about the relations. Krackhardt and Kilduff's (1999) survey of employees at four workplaces asked each informant to identify his or her friends among coworkers. They found a curvilinear relationship between network structure and perceived balance: employees perceived both their immediate friendship circle and their most peripheral contacts as more balanced than were those persons at intermediate distances. A major implication is that both close and distant ties can be subject to high informant bias, a topic addressed in the next section.

3.4. Informant Bias

We define *informant bias* as the discrepancy between self-reported and actual behaviors. Social scientists have long documented the gap between verbal and behavioral data. In the early 1930s, Richard LaPierre and a young Chinese couple traveled by car across the United States, eating at 184 restaurants and staying in 66 hotels, and were refused service by only one hotel. After the trip, LaPierre sent letters to all the establishments, asking whether they would "accept members of the Chinese race"; 92 percent replied "no" (LaPierre, 1934). LaPierre concluded that behavioral expressions of prejudicial attitudes required favorable conditions. In another study, Kronenfeld and Kronenfeld (1972) asked respondents who were leaving restaurants what the waiters and waitresses were wearing, and what kind of music was playing. Many respondents provided quite detailed information about the clothing and music, although none of the restaurants had waitpersons or played music.

Informant biases can result from various sources. Many informants cannot cognitively handle the large amounts of data required to report their behaviors accurately (Bernard, Killworth, Sailer, & Kronenfeld, 1984). Two other reasons are that informants cognitively impose a categorical form on noncategorical affiliation patterns (Freeman, 1992), and that informants correct their perceptions to maintain a balanced network among their close friends (Krackhardt & Kilduff, 1999). Some researchers argue that informant bias is not random noise; rather, some informants are better than others at providing accurate accounts of their actions. For example, some studies showed that familiarity with the interview topic can boost informant recall of events (Romney & Weller, 1984; Romney, Weller, & Batchelder, 1986). In contrast, another study found that, although informants with great knowledge about the topic forget very little, they also tend to create errors by reporting on nonexistent members (Freeman, Romney, & Freeman, 1987). Another analysis revealed that all informants tended to portray themselves as more central than was reported by other network participants. Thus, a group-level representation of a network may be more accurate than the individual-level reports (Kumbasar et al., 1994). Several recent studies have examined informant issues in research on egocentric networks (e.g., Brewer, 2000; Feld & Carter, 2002; Johnson & Orbach, 2002; White & Watkins, 2000).

Perhaps the most devastating news for social network researchers who use self-report data as proxies for network actors' behavioral data was a series of projects conducted by H. Russell Bernard and his associates (Bernard & Killworth, 1977; Bernard, Killworth, & Sailer, 1981; Bernard et al., 1984).

They constructed and compared seven sets of paired communication network datasets: cognitive data constructed from participants' self-reports, and behavioral data constructed by either a machine-monitoring system or "objective" observers' records. These datasets were two panels of deaf TTY users in the Washington, D.C., area; amateur operators from a radio wireless association in Virginia, Pennsylvania, and Ohio; employees in a social science research firm; a graduate program in technology education at West Virginia University; a college fraternity house; and a group of Electronic Information Exchange System (EIES) users. For example, the EIES users recorded self-report data (cognitive network) and data logged by the EIES electronic monitoring system (behavioral network). All seven paired network datasets included information on "who the respondent contacts and communicates with," "how often they communicate," and "how long they communicate." Comparing these cognitive and behavioral datasets, Bernard et al. (1981, p. 17) found that, on average, about half the informants' self-reports were erroneous in some ways, leading to a conclusion that

> People do not know, with any acceptable accuracy, to whom they talk over any given period of time. . . . We are now convinced that cognitive data about communication can not be used as proxy for the equivalent behavioral data.

Other scholars argued that the situation was not so hopeless as depicted by Bernard and his colleagues. Knoke and Kuklinski (1982, p. 32) challenged the accuracy and unobtrusiveness of the objective observers. They raised such questions as, "To what extent did the unobtrusive observer disrupt ongoing activities?," "How accurately was he able to record interactions?," and "What about interactions during the unobserved times?" Bernard et al. (1984) later moderated their stance, acknowledging that, despite some systematic distortion in cognitive data, facilitative factors could reduce informant biases, such as greater informant familiarity with cultural subjects or interviewers providing recall aid to informants. They suggested that "the evidence of informant inaccuracy ought not to lead to complaints or to despair. It ought to lead instead to a rich, relatively unexplored arena of research" (Bernard et al., 1984, p. 513).

Informant bias frequently occurs in other systematic ways. Biased informants perceive themselves as close to the center (Kumbasar et al., 1994), forget less-prominent players, falsely recall major actors in a network (Freeman et al., 1987), and cognitively correct their perceptions to force a balanced network between themselves and their close or distant friends (Krackhardt & Kilduff, 1999). Informant bias also commonly arises through inaccurate recall (Bernard et al., 1981; Bernard et al., 1984). Informants who fail to recall accurately make two typical errors: (1) forgetting persons with whom they have interacted, and (2) falsely recalling interactions that never occurred (Freeman et al., 1987). Moreover, forgetting and false recall are not random occurrences. Informants tend to forget infrequent participants and falsely recall frequent participants. Freeman et al. (1987) recorded university faculty and students who attended nine colloquia. Five days after the last two meetings, the researchers surveyed 17 informants who attended and 16 informants who did not attend those meetings but had attended at least two prior sessions. Informants were asked who was present and absent at the meetings. The informants made 141 errors (115 forgetting and 26 false recall) out of 272 opportunities ($17 \times 16 = 272$). The error rate of 52 percent was very close to Bernard et al.'s (1981) estimate that half of informant self-reports are inaccurate. The colloquium informants varied in their knowledge of other attendees, which affected their error rates (Freeman et al., 1987, p. 312). Compared to less-knowledgeable informants (who interacted with other attendees only at the colloquia), more-knowledgeable informants (who knew others from a broad spectrum of settings) were less likely to forget but more likely to commit false recall. Thus, contrary to conventional wisdom that knowledgeable informants provide accurate accounts, they were actually prone to false recall. However, the persons falsely recalled by the high-knowledgeable informants were the more frequent attendees. Because a major concern in social research is measuring patterns of repeated activities, high-knowledge people are good informants for collecting such data (Freeman et al., 1987).

High levels of agreement between informants often indicate low levels of bias and greater informant validity. In this vein, Romney et al. (1986) proposed a consensus model to link informant competency (the extent to which informants know the subject) with informant consensus and informant validity. A central argument is "the correspondence between the answers of any two informants is a function of the extent to which each is correlated with the truth" (p. 316). In other words, valid respondents tend to produce the same answers more often than invalid respondents. The researchers required informants to respond to a set of questions, to which only the researchers had the answer keys. They constructed each informant's "true" validity level, measured as the proportion of correct answers divided by total answers, and consensus validity level, estimated from a consensus formula. They found high correlations between informants' true accuracy and their consensus accuracy, leading to a conclusion that consensus answers are almost equivalent to valid answers.

In summary, contrary to Bernard et al.'s (1981) declaration that informant self-reports erroneously reflect actual events, research on informant bias provides fruitful advice regarding how to use informants wisely. Highly knowledgeable informants produce unbiased data about long-term repeated patterns. They also tend to produce consensus answers to questions, which indicates greater validity. Individuals' perceptions are biased toward portraying themselves as more central in a network than does the systematic aggregation of all network actors' perceptions. Thus, systematic perceptions should be a better indicator of people's locations in a network than are these individuals' self-reports. In addition, egos tend to be biased about their close friends and distant contacts by activating the "balanced schema" in making reports. Researchers using an egocentric approach to collecting network data should adopt some corrective measures when analyzing close ties and distant relations.

3.5. Reliability

In the most general terms, *reliability* measures the extent to which a particular instrument, when applied repeatedly to the same subject, yields an identical result every time. Several reliability measures are available, including interobserver reliability, test-retest reliability, and internal consistency reliability, which subsumes split-half reliability and Cronbach's alpha (α) reliability (Neuman, 2000, pp. 178–185). Social network researchers often use test-retest methods to evaluate informant reliability. For example, informants nominate or check off the names of all persons with whom they discuss important matters. The retest repeats the same request to the same informants at a later time. Comparing the level of agreement between the two sets of responses indicates each informant's reliability. A perfect correlation between the tests, where both times an informant names exactly the same persons with whom he or she discusses important matters, indicates complete reliability. In contrast, a complete disjoint answer, in which an informant chooses a completely different set of persons each time, suggests no reliability. A critical issue in executing the test-retest method is the interval between the tests. Differing answers between the two tests may reflect genuine changes in personal networks. Indeed, people continually develop new contacts to whom they can resort for some expressive or instrumental assistance, such as discussing important matters, house moving, child care, or borrowing money. Methodologists argue that this turnover problem can be attenuated by shortening the interval between the two reliability tests (Brewer, 2000). The shorter the interval, the less likely genuine changes in personal networks will occur, thus the less likely those changes are to be confounded with the reliability measure.

One simple and frequently used test-retest reliability measure is Jaccard's coefficient, the proportion of agreements after excluding joint negative pairs. It is calculated as the number of persons nominated by an informant at both times divided by the total number of unique nominations for both tests (Brewer, 2000). The Jaccard coefficient ranges from 0.00, indicating no reliability, to 1.00, indicating complete reliability. The following illustration involves a hypothetical checklist of 35 names, whose results appear in this crosstabulation, with cell frequencies conventionally labeled A–D:

	Second Interview	
First Interview	Names checked	Not checked
Names checked	A = 12	B = 5
Not checked	C = 3	D = 15

That is, at the first interview, the informant checked 17 names; the second interview yielded 15 nominations; and 12 persons were chosen at both interviews. Jaccard's coefficient $= A/(A + B + C) = 12/(12 + 5 + 3) = 0.60$. Because each informant in a group may have differing reliabilities, a group-level Jaccard coefficient would simply be the mean or median of the individual coefficients.

Informant reliability is often correlated with validity (Romney & Weller, 1984). If only a portion of informants' cognitive self-reports reflects their factual behaviors, the consensus among informants can often indicate the level of validity of informant recall. For example, in responding to questions about tennis games, tennis players should exhibit more consensuses among themselves than would non–tennis players. Players with complete knowledge would answer the questions with full consensus, whereas players with little knowledge would give very divergent answers. Drawing from this central argument, Romney and Weller (1984) reanalyzed Bernard et al.'s datasets to identify the factors distinguishing "good" informants, who are valid and reliable, from the "bad" informants, who are invalid and unreliable. They found that an individual's reliability, measured as the correlation between individual recall and aggregated recall at the group level, was positively associated with his or her validity, measured as the extent to which the individual's recall corresponds to the aggregated data. In addition, individuals with high reliability tend to have higher correlation in their self-reports than do individuals with low reliability. Therefore, the major finding is that, although reliability predicts validity, informants with high validity will have more similar responses to one another than will informants of low reliability. Further, the informants should be weighted by their reliability: The answers of more reliable informants should be taken more seriously than those of less reliable informants. To focus only on highly reliable persons, the informants in Bernard et al.'s data provided valid self-reports, indicated by a strong correspondence between their recall data and the observed aggregated interaction data (Romney & Weller, 1984, p. 75).

To the extent that forgetting relationships is inevitable among informants, aided recall procedures—such as checklists providing cues and prompts—pose a less-serious reliability problem than free recall methods, where informants must nominate candidates without such assistance. For instance, Jones and Fischer (1978) interviewed 86 people about such specific network relations as "borrowing money" and "discussing work-related matters." In the first interview, the informants freely recalled anyone in those networks. At the second interview, the researchers gave each informant a checklist and repeated the name-generator questions. The second interview elicited 34 percent more names than the first interview, and 27 percent of names mentioned at the initial interview were not checked in the later interview.

In another network reliability study, Brewer and Webster (1999) interviewed 217 residents of a university residence hall. The first interview asked informants to write down the names of all their friends living in the hall. The second interview provided a roster of all hall residents and asked informants again to identify all their friends. With the roster as a cue, informants named 20 percent more friends on average. The previously forgotten names tended to be more distant friends, suggesting that, without cues and prompts, informants tend to forget their less-intimate alters. One inference is that substantial unreliability would occur whenever a researcher compares free recall to aided recall data gathered at separate informant interviews. In this case, low reliability only indicates greater validity: Informants produce a more complete list of nominations in one interview than in the other. Of course, reliability does not ensure validity. An informant might produce identical nominees at both times, thus achieving perfect reliability, yet each interview could be biased by consistently omitting many nominees. Nevertheless, highly valid network responses typically have high reliability. That is, if an informant can always enumerate all friends in response to a specific name generator, that informant also likely produces a consistent set of friends at different interview times.

Due to the unique characteristics of social network data, particularly in egocentric analyses, informant reliability and validity measures differ greatly from conventional measures for other types of data (Marsden, 1993). In egocentric samples drawn from small, closed communities, ego-informants often nominate many of the same alters on a specific relation. High correlations among informants in choosing similar alters indicates high informant reliability. Similarly, high informant validity is implied by high correlations of an informant's descriptions of his or her alters' characteristics (e.g., their ages, genders, educations, statuses) and the alters' self-reports of those characteristics. (This interpretation presumes that all alters' attributes are available from self-reports to serve as factual data for comparison with the ego-informant's descriptions.)

A panel survey of contraceptive discussion networks among women in Kenyan villages exemplified this ego-network approach to reliability and validity (White & Watkins, 2000). The researchers interviewed 925 women in December, 1994, and reinterviewed 743 one year later. The informants were asked both times, "With whom have you chatted about family planning?" Informants then reported about the age, education, wealth, and use of family planning of four randomly selected alters. The researchers also asked every alter to report her own age, education, wealth, and family planning. White and Watkins found that the greatest discrepancy between the ego and alter reports occurred for the alters' uses of family planning. In contrast, agreements tended to be highest on some directly observable conditions, such as "whether alters have a metal roof" and "whether alters have a sofa set." Moreover, the reports about alters by informants who cited the same alters correlated only $r = .31$, just a bit higher than the mean correlation of the egos' reports with the alters' self-reports (.25). These findings show that informant knowledge about alters' family planning is neither reliable nor valid. Only 18 percent of the alters named by informants in the first panel were cited again in the second panel, indicating either low reliability or much network instability during the intervening year.

3.6. Missing Data

Social network studies are especially sensitive to missing data. In egocentric data collection, an ego with N alters is asked to report on C_N^2 nondirected dyadic relations. Specifically, $C_N^2 = \frac{N!}{2! \times (N-2)!}$ where $N!$ (pronounced "N factorial") is the product of all the positive integers from 1 to N. For example, if ego has five alters, $C_5^2 = \frac{5!}{2! \times (5-2)!} = \frac{(1 \times 2 \times 3 \times 4 \times 5)}{(1 \times 2) \times (1 \times 2 \times 3)} = \frac{120}{12} = 10$; therefore, ego must give information on ten nondirected ties. For directed relations, the number of ties among ego's alters is twice as large: $2\ C_N^2$; in the example, ego would have to report on 20 directed ties. The relational response rate (R) for egocentric networks is calculated by dividing the number of reported ties by the total number of possible dyadic relations among the alters. For example, if ego reported about 8 of the 10 nondirected relations, then $R = 0.80$, or 80 percent; if ego failed to report on 6 of the 20 directed relations, then $R = 0.70$, or 70 percent.

Calculating the response rate for a complete social network is more complicated. A complete network consists of the dyadic relations among all pairs of the N actors in the network. For a nondirected network, R is less attenuated because a report by one member of a dyad suffices when the measure is reliable. For example, to measure friendship between actors A and B, information provided by either informant could be used to determine whether that relation is present or absent. That is, unless both A's and B's reports about one another are missing, we measure their friendship with a single report. In general, for a complete nondirected network of N actors with no alter reports from M actors, the response rate for a particular relation is calculated as:

$$R \begin{cases} = 100 \text{ percent when } M = 0 \text{ or } M = 1 \\ = \left(1 - \dfrac{C_M^2}{C_N^2}\right) \times 100 \text{ percent when } 1 < M < N \\ = 0 \text{ percent when } M = N \end{cases}$$

For example, in a network of five actors, the nodal response rate and the relational response rate for varied numbers of missing nodes are the following:

Number of Missing Nodes	Nodal Response Rate	Relational Response Rate
0	100%	100%
1	80%	100%
2	60%	90%
3	40%	70%
4	20%	40%
5	0%	0%

To illustrate, assume that the network's five actors are labeled A, B, C, D, and E. The 10 nondirected dyadic relations among these five actors are AB, AC, AD, AE, BC, BD, BE, CD, CE, and DE. If actor A fails to report its relations, those dyadic ties can be obtained from the other four actors' reports about A. Thus, the relational response rate is 100 percent despite missing reports from one node. When the missing nodes range between 2 and 4 $(1 < M < N)$, the relational response rate is $(1 - \frac{C_M^2}{C_N^2}) \times 100$ percent. For example, if three nodes (A, B, and C) do not report their relations with anyone, the response rate is 70 percent $[(1 - \frac{C_3^2}{C_5^2}) \times 100 = 70\%]$. In this case, three nondirected relations are missing (AB, AC, and BC), but the other seven dyads are reported by at least one member. If no actors provide information, both nodal and relational response rates fall to 0 percent. Because the nodal response rate is computed as $(1 - \frac{M}{N}) \times 100$ and $\frac{M}{N}$ is always greater than $\frac{C_M^2}{C_N^2}$ (a mathematical proof is available upon request to the authors), the relational response rates for nondirected networks are always higher than the nodal response rates at every level of missing nodal reports.

In contrast, missing nodal information has a substantial impact on the relational response rates of directed networks. Asymmetries occur in many types of ties, such as giving advice, trusting, and liking. Actors A and B have two directed relations: AB denotes A's report of its relation to B and BA represents B's reports of its relation to A. Therefore, each missing node results in missing relational information about that node's ties directed toward all other actors. Assuming a network of N actors with M missing nodes, the relational response rate for a directed network is the following:

$$R \begin{cases} = 100 \text{ percent when } M = 0 \\ = \left(1 - \frac{M \times (N-1)}{2 \times C_N^2}\right) \times 100 \text{ percent when } 0 < M < N \\ = 0 \text{ percent when } M = N \end{cases}$$

To demonstrate, the five-actor network has $(5^2 - 5) = 20$ directed dyadic relations: AB, BA, AC, CA, AD, DA, AE, EA, BC, CB, BD, DB, BE, EB, CD, DC, CE, EC, DE, and ED. If every actor reports its relations with all others, we obtain a 100 percent relational response rate. If one node (e.g., A) is missing, all of A's reports are also missing, resulting in four unreported relations (AB, AC, AD, and AE) among the 20 dyadic relations, a response rate of 80 percent. Because each node in a directed network must assess its relations with the other nodes, M missing nodes $(0 < M < N)$ generate $M \times (N-1)$ missing relations. Of course, when no nodes report any relations $(M = N)$, both nodal and relational response rates equal 0 percent.

With a bit of arithmetic deduction, we now prove that relational response rate always equals nodal response rate in a directed network. Suppose we have a directed network of N nodes and M missing nodes; the nodal response rate is $(1 - \frac{M}{N})$, whereas the relational response rate is $(1 - \frac{M \times (N-1)}{2 \times C_N^2})$. In particular, $\frac{M \times (N-1)}{2 \times C_N^2} = M \times (N-1) \div (2 \times \frac{N!}{2! \times (N-2)!}) = \frac{M \times (N-1)}{N \times (N-1)} = \frac{M}{N}$. Thus, in a directed network with five nodes, the response rate for both nodes and relations are 100 percent with no missing node, 80 percent with one missing node, 60 percent with two missing nodes, 40 percent with three missing nodes, 20 percent with four missing nodes, and 0 percent with all five missing nodes.

In the preceding discussion, we argued that a report by one member of a dyad in a nondirected network could be treated as a reliable measure of the dyadic relation. Scholars typically assert that this practice must be exercised with great caution because nonreciprocal relations often occur (Stork & Richards, 1992). For example, in a communication network, person A reports talking with person B, but B claims never to talk with A. This contradiction calls into question the practice of reconstructing the relation between a responding actor and a missing actor from information provided only by a nonmissing node. Stork and Richards (1992) suggested that similarity in a pair of actors' characteristics, such as their age, sex, and education, may be a good indicator of their dyadic tie confirmation. In addition, network reliability, measured as the proportion of all dyadic relations described identically by both members, indicates how well a single report characterizes the link between respondents and nonrespondents. When network reliability is high and both members of a dyad have identical or very similar characteristics, one member's report should serve as a reliable proxy for their relation. Kossinets (2003) endorsed Stork and Richards's method of reconstructing a dyadic tie from the respondent actor's report, provided that the overall number of nonrespondents is low.

Egocentric network studies are vulnerable to missing data because people often fail to describe ties among their alters. Researching the 1985 GSS discussion networks, Burt (1987) reported that the missing data for the GSS egocentric studies are less severe: among the total 1,534 respondents who enumerate 4,483 discussion partners, only 66 respondents provided incomplete network data involving 195 discussion partners. Burt compared two kinds of discussion partners—those with complete network data and those with only partial network data. He found that 35 percent of the former group's alters were not close to any other alters, as reported by the respondent, but that figure increased to 59 percent for the latter group. The major implication is that the missing relations among alters in an egocentric network tend to be weak ties. Egos seem more likely to report relations for alters perceived as well connected to other alters than they are to report relations for alters who are seen as isolated. This finding also explains why, contrary to other methodological research, the college-educated GSS respondents produced more incomplete egocentric network data than the less-educated respondents. College graduates tended to enumerate egocentric networks consisting of many weakly tied alters, which in turn engendered more missing reports about these alters' relations.

As no foolproof *post facto* remedy to the missing data problem exists, the solution to this problem lies in convincing more respondents of the importance of participating in the research (Knoke & Kuklinski, 1982, p. 35). To elicit higher participation, such as the 90 percent response rate achieved by some network studies, extraordinary research efforts often require a combination of different persuasion techniques such as personal letters, phone contacts, and monetary inducements. The missing data problem is not a unique plague on social network studies using survey methods. Archival studies, for example, are also susceptible to the curse of missing data. Granted, the completeness of archival data is at the mercy of the data repository's maintenance practices. However, given a certain level of data availability, the competency of the coders and the efficacy of the software in data mining can also make a substantial difference in the amount and quality of information extracted. Poorly trained coders and ill-designed software definitely contribute to sizable amounts of missing data.

CHAPTER 4
BASIC METHODS FOR ANALYZING NETWORKS

This chapter discusses basic methods for analyzing social networks, giving equal attention to traditionally important topics and recent developments. In particular, we review density, centrality, cohesiveness, structural equivalence, clustering, multidimensional scaling, and blockmodels. Because representing network data always precedes analyzing social networks, this chapter naturally starts with a description of two distinct, but closely related, methods for representing and analyzing social network data: graphs and matrices. Graphs present visualizations of social networks, whereas matrices use mathematical algebraic representations of network relations. Although social network scholars may freely choose either graphs or matrices to present their data, both methods have their respective advantages and disadvantages. Graphs provide much more forceful visual illustrations of network structures but do not support mathematical manipulations. In contrast, although matrices are less user-friendly, they facilitate sophisticated mathematical and computer analyses of social network data. Network analysts must become proficient at routinely applying both sets of tools to conceptualize and measure key features of their relational data.

4.1. Graphs

Jacob Moreno's (1934) pioneering sociometric techniques emphasized constructing a *sociogram*, a two-dimensional diagram for displaying the relations among actors in a bounded social system, for example, an elementary school classroom. Points and lines, the two primitive elements of a sociogram, also define a *graph*, thus allowing applications of concepts and theorems from graph theory (Harary, 1969). In sociograms and graphs, actors are represented by a set of *N points* (also called *nodes* or *vertices*), often labeled by identifying names, letters, or numbers. A line (also called an *arc* or *edge*) drawn between a pair of points indicates a relation or tie; the absence of a line means no direct relation exists between the two actors. Two nodes are *adjacent* if a line exists between them; a node is *incident* to a line (and vice versa) if it is one of the two nodes defining the line. The precise placement of nodes and lengths of lines in a network diagram is somewhat arbitrary, although some versions may be clearer than others. Constructing insightful sociograms is as much an artistic as a scientific activity.

If a line has no arrowhead, the relation is *nondirected* or mutual (e.g., coworkers). If relations are directed from one actor to another, the result is a *directed graph* or *digraph*. Formally, a digraph is a finite set of nodes and a set of ordered pairs (a, b), where node a is the initial node of the line and b is the terminal node. A single-headed arrow indicates a *directed tie*, from the actor at the tail to the actor at the arrowhead (e.g., giving advice). A line with arrowheads at both ends indicates two directed ties, from each dyad member to the other, which suggests reciprocity or mutuality (e.g., each actor chooses the other as a "close friend"). An alternative format uses two single-headed arrows, each pointing in the other's direction. Some sociograms may vary the thickness of lines, or apply different types of dashes, for a visual display of the strength, intensity, or frequency of dyadic interactions.

To illustrate the graphic representation of a social network structure, we draw from network research by Feldman-Savelsberg et al. (2005) on Cameroon women's hometown associations. To analyze how collective memory affects the women's discussion of reproduction, Feldman-Savelsberg et al. (2005) interviewed 156 women belonging to six women's associations in Yaounde, Cameroon. Their in-depth interviews contained questions about the women's social networks, such as "Please rank the strength of ties between you and other women in the same association according to the following schema: (1) confidants, (2) friends, (3) acquaintances, and (4) complete strangers." As each woman was asked only to rank her ties with other women belonging to the same association, separate network structures were constructed for each of the six associations. For a concise illustration, we use only the network structure of Association 6, which has six members.

Figure 4.1 shows the graph of social relations among the members of Association 6. Line thickness indicates three rank choices, with no line indicating total strangers. Of the 23 directed ties among the six women, only 4 of the 15 dyads are mutually agreed (both women chose the same rank): Women 1 and 2 rank each other as confidants, Women 3 and 5 are friends, Women 2 and 5 are acquaintances, and Women 5 and 6 are total strangers. The other 11 pairs have different rankings on their relations. For

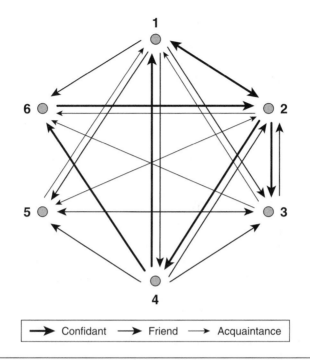

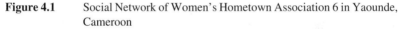

Figure 4.1   Social Network of Women's Hometown Association 6 in Yaounde, Cameroon

example, Woman 6 ranks Woman 2 as a confidant, but Woman 2 considers Woman 6 a mere acquaintance. Although sociograms may present intuitive and straightforward pictures of network structures, they often provide poor visual illustration for large networks consisting of tens or even hundreds of actors. We can see that with only six actors and 23 directed relations, the graph appears to be overwhelmingly entangled. In contrast, a matrix can easily display network relations for dozens of actors.

Several basic concepts can be illustrated with the artificial seven-actor digraph in Figure 4.2, which could represent an advice-giving sociogram. A *subgraph* is a subset of nodes and lines within a larger graph. The triad (Tom, Betty, Jane) is a subgraph. A *walk* is an alternating sequence of incident nodes and lines, in which each node is incident with its preceding and following lines. A *walk length* is the number of lines it contains. The walk Jane-Tom-Betty-Harry-Dick-Sally has length 5. A *trail* is a walk consisting of distinct lines, although some nodes may be visited more than once: Dick-Sally-Harry-Tom-Betty-Harry-Dick is a trail of length 6. Because that trail

48

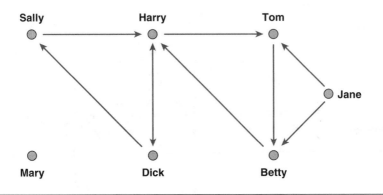

Figure 4.2   A Seven-Actor Directed Network

begins and ends at the same node, it is also a *circuit*. Wasserman and Faust (1994, pp. 107–108) discuss the related concepts of closed walks, tours, and cycles.

In network analysis, a very important concept is the *path*, defined as a walk with entirely distinct nodes and lines (no node or line can be included more than once). In digraphs, paths must follow a sequence of distinct nodes where each line originates at the preceding node. In other words, all arrows point in one direction. Thus, Betty-Harry-Sally is not a path, but Betty-Harry-Dick-Sally is. The length of a path (the number of lines in its walk) is its *path distance*. Several paths may exist between two nodes, but the shortest path between them is the *geodesic*. Of the two paths from Jane to Sally, the geodesic (Jane-Betty-Harry-Dick-Sally) has path distance 4, which is shorter than the path Jane-Tom-Betty-Harry-Dick-Sally, whose distance is 5. *What is the geodesic from Dick to Tom?*

Two nodes are said to be *reachable* if at least one path of any length exists between them. Tom is reachable from Sally; although Jane is not reachable by Sally, Sally is reachable by Jane.

A graph is *connected* if paths exist between every pair of nodes, but is *disconnected* if at least one pair has no path between them. A node that has no lines connecting it to any other node is an *isolate*; Mary is obviously isolated from the other six, and therefore the graph is disconnected. If we ignore Mary, the remaining six-actor digraph may exhibit one of three levels of connectedness:

Strongly connected: every pair of nodes is connected by directed paths in both directions (i.e., from *a* to *b* and from *b* to *a*).

Unilaterally connected: all pairs are linked by a path in one direction but not the other direction.

Weakly connected: all pairs are joined by lines disregarding their direction.

Clearly, the six-actor digraph is only weakly connected. However, subsets of actors within a larger network may be more connected than is the entire graph. A *graph component* is a maximal subgraph that forms a connected graph, whereas a strongly connected component is a maximal subgraph forming a strongly connected graph. The subgraph Sally-Dick-Harry-Tom-Betty is a unilaterally connected component because directed paths of varying lengths connect every pair in one direction. This component is maximal because adding Jane would destroy unilateral connectedness. *Why is even the small Jane-Tom-Betty subgraph neither a strong nor a unilateral component?*

In a connected graph, a node is a *cutpoint* if its removal would disconnect the graph, that is, create two or more components. If Harry is removed from Figure 4.2, the six-node graph falls into two smaller components (Sally-Dick and Tom-Betty-Jane). Similarly, if removing one line would disconnect a graph into two or more components, that line is a *bridge. Does the diagram contain a bridge? Why?*

Networks with cutpoints or bridges may be more vulnerable to disruption than networks with many redundant paths that sustain information and resource flows. For example, networks of covert terrorist cells may be destabilized by the capture or killing of a key player (Borgatti, 2003; Tsvetovat & Carley, 2005).

4.2. Matrices

An algebraic representation of network relations can express all the quantitative information embedded in a sociogram, while enabling a much larger set of analyses than possible with the corresponding visual representation. The basic form of social network data for mathematical analysis is a tabular display, the *sociomatrix* (also called *adjacency matrix*), typically a square array of numerical elements arranged in rows and columns. For example, the capital boldface notation $\mathbf{X}(N, N)$ represents sociomatrix $\mathbf{X}$ with dimensions of N rows and N columns and whose N^2 *cells* display information about the relations among the N social actors. The sequence or order of the actors is identical across the rows and the columns, with subscripts i and j, ranging from 1 to N, respectively referring to a particular row-and-column location. In general, the value of a cell is denoted x_{ij}; for example, x_{35}

indicates the value in the third row, fifth column of a sociomatrix. In most substantive social network applications, the values of the matrix main diagonal (cells in the ith row, ith column) are not meaningful—for example, a person cannot be his or her own close friend—and are ignored during data analyses. Consequently, the maximum number of unique cell values in a sociomatrix of N actors is $N^2 - N$.

The numerical value in a sociomatrix cell measures a specific relationship between the pair of actors designated by the corresponding row and column. By convention, for directed relations, the actors in the rows are initiators or senders and the actors in the columns are terminators or receivers of the relation. The most basic measurement is the presence or absence of a tie, a dichotomy indicated by binary values of 1 and 0, respectively. Thus, the binary matrix entry $x_{ij} = 1$ indicates that actor i sends a relation to actor j, whereas $x_{ij} = 0$ denotes no relation sent by i to j. Because relations in a digraph are not constrained to be mutual or reciprocal, their matrices are *asymmetric*. In nondirected networks, $x_{ij} = x_{ji}$; that is, the value of the relation between sender i and receiver j always equals the value between sender j and receiver i. Such matrices are *symmetric*.

Sociomatrices may include nonbinary values, reflecting the intensity of relations, such as frequency of contacts, tie strength, or magnitude of associations. In such *valued graphs*, the cell entries could vary from 0 to some maximum level of dyadic interaction, or might include decimals or even negative values to represent adverse relations, such as "dislikes" or "enemy."

Table 4.1 displays the matrix representation of Hometown Association 6 at Yaounde, Cameroon. This matrix is an algebraic translation of the graph in Figure 4.1. Because each woman ranked the strength of her relation with the other five women, and disagreements could occur in a dyad's evaluations, the matrix is valued and asymmetric. The women listed in the rows provide evaluations of their ties to the others, while the women in the columns are the evaluated targets. (The row and column labels are not part of the matrix, but are included for reference.) For example, Woman 1 ranks her tie with Woman 3 at strength 2 (friend), but Woman 3 ranks her tie with Woman 1 only at strength 1 (acquaintance). Dashes indicate that the values on the main diagonal are not meaningful. Table 4.2 is the binary matrix corresponding to the seven-actor graph in Figure 4.2.

Sometimes network researchers use nonsquare matrices to indicate actor attributes or their participation in certain events. A mathematical notation $\mathbf{Z}(N, M)$ denotes a rectangular matrix $\mathbf{Z}$ in which N is the number of actors and M is the number of attributes, events, or locations. For example, Freeman and Webster (1994) observed 43 regular beach-goers over 31 days, recording 353 events in which these people could be involved (e.g., picnics, games). They created a 43 by 353 matrix, in which an entry of 1 for row i

TABLE 4.1.
Sociomatrix of Women's Hometown Association 6 in Yaounde, Cameroon

	W1	W2	W3	W4	W5	W6
W1	–	3	2	2	2	2
W2	3	–	3	3	1	1
W3	1	2	–	0	2	1
W4	3	2	2	–	2	3
W5	1	1	2	0	–	0
W6	0	3	0	0	0	–

0 = complete stranger; 1 = acquaintance; 2 = friend; 3 = confidant.

and column j indicated that person i participated in event j. If a researcher collects network data on more than one type of relation, then multiple sociomatrices can be constructed and analyzed jointly or separately. The matrix notation to designate a particular relation among R *multiplex* networks simply adds a third subscript; that is, x_{ijk} is the cell value in the ith row and jth column of the kth relational matrix.

4.3. Relationship Measures

Basic relationship measures for social network data include density and centrality. Before discussing them, we review some network data fundamentals, distinguished along two dimensions: directionality and valuation. Directionality separates social network data into nondirected and directed relations. In nondirected relational data, the initiators and recipients (e.g., senders and receivers; choosers and chosen) in a dyad are indistinguishable: If Dick is married to Jane, then Jane is also married to Dick. Other types of nondirected ties include comembership in an organization, joint attendance at a social event, and mutual knowledge. To collect data on nondirected relations, researchers often only need to ask one informant and use that response to indicate the dyadic tie. In contrast, directed relations occur when either member of a dyad may initiate a relation with the other member, thus resulting in four possible binary combinations: (1) Person A gives something (e.g., information, advice, money) to Person B, but B doesn't give to A; (2) B gives to A, but not the reverse; (3) both A and B exchange with one another; and (4) neither A nor B transacts. Directed data are typically collected as egos' subjective reports about some network relation, which could disagree with their alters' views of the same relation. Many types of network data that might be theorized as nondirected relations ought to be measured as directed-tie data. For instance, to assess the presence of a

TABLE 4.2.
Sociomatrix of Seven-Actor Direct Network in Figure 4.2

	Sally	Harry	Dick	Tom	Betty	Jane	Mary
Sally	–	1	0	0	0	0	0
Harry	0	–	1	1	0	0	0
Dick	1	1	–	0	0	0	0
Tom	0	0	0	–	1	0	0
Betty	0	1	0	0	–	0	0
Jane	0	0	0	1	1	–	0
Mary	0	0	0	0	0	0	–

trust relationship, researchers should ask both parties whether they trust one another. Rather than assuming that friendship ties are always reciprocal, analysts could treat them as inherently directional: Ted may consider Sally to be his friend, but Sally doesn't think of Ted as her friend. Many cognitive social structure network relations, as discussed in Chapter 3, are inherently directional, because they consist of actors' reports about subjective beliefs, attitudes, or perceptions of relations, which are likely to diverge from the alters' subjective views. Even when a relation is theoretically conceptualized as nondirected, researchers usually should err on the side of caution by asking both members of a dyad to provide separate reports. Differences can be reconciled during subsequent analyses, using either a weak criterion (e.g., a tie exists if at least one member reports it) or a strong criterion (both members must confirm the tie). Data collection that preserves this option enables analysts to assess the robustness of their results under alternative measurement assumptions.

Depending on how much information is available on a relation, social network ties can be measured as binary or valued scales. In binary data, respondents only indicate the presence (coded 1) or absence (coded 0) of a tie between a pair of actors. In valued data, they not only indicate the presence or absence of a tie but also rank or otherwise quantify the intensity or frequency of their interactions. For example, adolescents could be asked to estimate the number of times they had sexual relations with each partner during the preceding year. Thus, binary network data have only two values, 0 or 1. But valued relational data represent an ordinal or continuous scale, ranging from 0 to a potentially very large maximum value, and could encompass decimal places or proportions.

Crosstabulating the directionality and valuation dimensions generates four basic types of social network data: binary nondirected, binary directed, valued nondirected, and valued directed ties. Binary nondirected data demand the least information from respondents or informants. Interviewers need to ask only one member of a dyad to indicate the presence or absence of a tie. Valued nondirected data require one person to quantify the relation between both members. Binary directed measures require only that both persons mention the occurrence of a tie. But valued directed data need the most detailed information, two reports about the magnitude of the dyadic relation. Because egocentric network research and complete network studies differ so drastically in their research design, sampling, data analyses, and interpretations, the following two subsections discuss measures applicable to these four types of network data.

Egocentric Network Measures. In egocentric network studies, informants are asked to report the alters with whom they have a specified relation. The relation is explicitly stated in the name-generator instructions given to survey respondents. A well-known example is the General Social Survey "discuss important matters" name generator, described in Chapter 3. No independent information was collected from any alters named by the 1985 GSS ego respondents. This subsection focuses on density and network range measures for egocentric networks.

Density measures the extent to which the N alters in an egocentric network are connected among themselves (omitting ego, to whom all alters are directly connected by definition). Assuming that relations are nondirected binary (present/absent) ties, the density (D) measure is the ratio of the number of reported dyadic ties (L) among the alters divided by the maximum possible dyadic ties:

$$D = \frac{L}{C_N^2}$$

where $C_N^2 = \frac{N!}{2! \times (N-2)!}$. For example, suppose ego has five alters and reports only two relations among them. Because $C_5^2 = \frac{5!}{2! \times (5-2)!} = \frac{(1 \times 2 \times 3 \times 4 \times 5)}{(1 \times 2) \times (1 \times 2 \times 3)} = \frac{120}{12} = 10$, the density is $D = \frac{L}{C_N^2} = \frac{2}{10} = 0.20$ or 20 percent.

If the ties in an egocentric network are measured as binary directed relations, the density formula is modified to the following:

$$D = \frac{L}{2 \times C_N^2}$$

The first difference in the two density formulas lies in the denominator, because a directed-tie egocentric network must have twice as many ordered pairs as a nondirected ego-centered network with the same N. The second difference is in the numerator. Although both numerators reflect the actual presence of dyadic ties, the latter must examine two relational directions. In binary nondirected network data, each connected dyad is counted just once, whereas in a binary directed network every dyad is counted twice because ego reports whether each alter initiates relations with the other member of the pair.

Next, assuming that the network data are valued nondirected relations, egocentric density is the following:

$$D = \frac{\sum L_w}{C_N^2}$$

In this formula, the numerator sums all the values attached to the ties that are present. Dividing the numerator by the maximum number of possible ties among N actors, this density measure reflects the average strength of the relations among ego's alters. Suppose a study asks ego to rank its five alters (A, B, C, D, and E) according to the following schema: no relations (0), acquaintance (1), friend (2), and confidant (3). If ego ranks A as a confidant of B, D as a friend of E, and no relations among all other dyads, then density $= (2 + 3)/10 = 0.5$, which means that the 10 egocentric network relations carry an average strength or weight of 0.5.

The last density measure applies to valued directed egocentric data:

$$D = \frac{\sum L_w}{2 \times C_N^2}$$

Its numerator sums up all the values attached to the perceived links, whereas the denominator reflects the maximum number of possible dyadic directed ties in a network of N actors, which is twice as many as a nondirected network of N actors.

The density measures in binary network data are restricted to proportions between 0, indicating no alter is connected to any other member of ego's network, and 1, indicating that all alters are directly connected to one another. This restriction occurs because the numerator for binary network density cannot be larger than the denominator. For both nondirected and directed binary egocentric data, the number of ties among dyads must be less than or equal to the maximum number of possible dyads. ($L \leq C_N^2$ when L only counts the presence of the ties and $L \leq 2 \times C_N^2$ when L takes into account both the presence and the directions of the ties.) However, for valued egocentric data, density can exceed 1.00, because the values assigned to relations among the dyads may be much larger than the maximum relational value of 1 for binary data.

Network range is broadly defined as the extent to which an actor's network links it to diverse other actors (Burt, 1983). In practice, researchers measure network range with a set of empirical indicators such as network size, density, and diversity (Campbell, Marsden, & Hurlbert, 1986). In particular, egocentric network diversity measures the extent of the heterogeneity of social characteristics of the alters in an ego's network. Depending on the level of measurement of alters' characteristics, egocentric diversity can be measured by the standard deviation for continuous variables or by the index of qualitative variation for categoric (discrete or ordered) variables.

When an alter characteristic is measured as a continuous variable, the standard deviation reveals the attribute's diversity within an egocentric network. In general, for the ith ego with N alters, where the jth alter's characteristic X_{ij} is a continuous variable, the standard deviation is the following:

$$s_{X_i} = \sqrt{\frac{\sum\limits_{J=1}^{N} (X_{ij} - \overline{X})^2}{N-1}}.$$

The mean of the standard deviations for all egos measures the attribute's diversity in a sample of egocentric networks. Marsden (1987) found that the mean standard deviation of alters' years of schooling for the 1985 General Social Survey was only 1.37 years, indicating that the alters in American core discussion networks tended to have similar levels of education.

When an alter characteristic is measured as a categoric variable, the index of qualitative variation (IQV) measures egocentric network diversity. In general, for the ith ego with N alters, where the alters are classified into K discrete or ordered categories, the IQV is

$$IQV_i = \frac{1 - \sum\limits_{j=1}^{K} p_j^2}{(K-1)/K}$$

where p_j^2 is the proportion of alters in the jth category. The IQV is standardized between 0.00, indicating that all N cases are in one category, and 1.00, indicating that alters are equally spread over the K categories. For example, if an ego names four men and one woman as alters, the sex composition IQV is $\frac{1-[(0.8)^2+(0.2)^2]}{(2-1)/2} = 0.64$, whereas someone naming three male and two female alters has a sex composition IQV of 0.96. Thus, the latter egocentric network exhibits greater gender diversity. The mean IQV across all egos constitutes a categoric variable's index of qualitative diversity for a sample. Using this approach, Marsden (1987) reported that the sex IQV for American egocentric network was 0.68, whereas the IQV for race was only 0.05. Clearly, the alters in Americans' core discussion groups were much more evenly balanced in their gender composition than in their racial diversity.

Complete Network Measures. In egocentric network studies, an ego constructs its network by enumerating the alters with whom he or she has a specific relationship. Unless sampled from a dense community, in which egos and alters are all well connected (White & Watkins, 2000), one ego's alters rarely overlap with another's. Therefore, the density measures discussed in the preceding paragraphs are based on the attributes of alters associated with unconnected informants. In contrast, in complete network studies, a researcher imposes a network boundary and focuses only on ties among actors in that population. For example, in Krackhardt's (1987) study of 21 high-tech managers in an organization, each person was asked to identify from whom among the other 20 managers they sought advice. Data collected using a complete network design consist of ties only among the selected actors; usually, ties to actors outside the network boundary are excluded. Therefore, applying one of the density measures for egocentric networks, discussed in the preceding section, produces a single value for a complete network. To illustrate, a random sample of N actors yields N egocentric density values, because each actor's egocentric network is different from the others. In contrast, a complete network has a single density value for the whole group, regardless of the population N. Despite this difference in level of analysis, the computation formulas for the four density measures are identical for both egocentric and complete networks.

In addition to density, other relationship measurements applicable to complete networks broadly include nodal degree, walks, trials, paths, cycles, components, geodesic distances, diameters, cutpoints, bridges, trees, and isomorphic subgraphs. Elaborating on all these measures goes beyond the scope of this book; see Wasserman and Faust (1994) for details. Instead, we discuss two fundamental topics: nodal degree and geodesics. These measures can be equally applied to complete networks and to egocentric networks. To facilitate exposition, we refer to four diagrams representing differing types of network data.

Nodal degree, $d(N_i)$, is the total number of relations of the ith actor (i.e., node), where degree refers to number of lines. In the binary nondirected graph in Figure 4.3, the nodal degrees of each actor are $d(N_A) = 4$, $d(N_B) = d(N_C) = d(N_D) = d(N_E) = 3$. The mean nodal degree of the complete network, obtained by summing the actors' nodal degrees and dividing by the number of actors, indicates the extent of connections among nodes. For Figure 4.3, the mean nodal degree $\frac{4+3+3+3+3}{5} = 3.2$.

For directed graphs, however, researchers must distinguish nodal indegree and outdegree. *Nodal indegree* is the number of lines received by one actor from other actors. *Nodal outdegree* is the number of lines sent by an actor to others. Imagine that Figure 4.4 is a friendship nomination network, in which Person A named B and E as friends but no one mentioned A as a

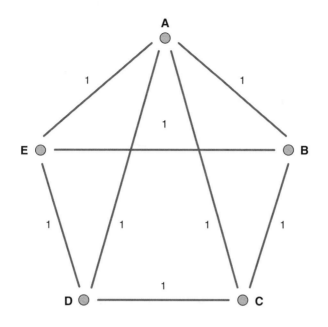

Figure 4.3   A Binary Nondirected Graph

friend. Thus, A's indegree is 0, but its outdegree is 2. Although an individual's indegree and outdegree may differ, the mean indegrees and outdegrees for a complete network are always equal, because the sum of lines coming into all actors is identical to the sum of lines originating from all actors. In Figure 4.4, the indegrees of actors A, B, C, D, and E are 0, 2, 1, 1, and 3, respectively, whereas their outdegrees are 2, 1, 1, 2, and 1. Both sets aggregate to 7; hence, the network's mean nodal degree is $\frac{7}{5} = 1.4$. Some scholars argue that outdegree in general suggests expansiveness, whereas indegree reflects receptivity or popularity (Wasserman & Faust, 1994, p. 126). In light of this intriguing suggestion, A is an expansive actor—choosing others as friends—yet is the least popular person in the network. In contrast, E is the most popular, but only a moderately expansive actor.

A review of network literature uncovered few suggestions for calculating the nodal degrees of valued graphs. One simplistic solution is to convert valued graphs by replacing all nonzero values to 1, then apply binary graph methods. This approach, however, throws away rich information about the strength of ties in valued graphs. Instead, we recommend a summation method for calculating the nodal degree of valued nondirected graphs,

58

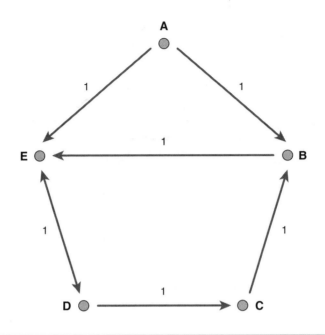

Figure 4.4   A Binary Directed Graph

which adds the values of all lines for an actor. Then, the mean nodal degree for a valued nondirected graph is the sum of all valued nodal degrees divided by the number of actors. The nodal degrees of A, B, C, D, and E in Figure 4.5 are 5, 13, 7, 5, and 12, respectively. The mean nodal degrees for this valued nondirected graph is $\frac{5+13+7+5+12}{5} = 8.4$. We acknowledge that the summation method can produce high nodal degree values for two contrasting scenarios: an actor with many lines of low value or one with only a few lines of high value. For example, consider a friendship network whose line values indicate the strength of the friend ties. The first scenario suggests a person having many shallow friends, whereas the second scenario implies a person with only a few close friends. The summation method produces identically high values for both node degrees, yet cannot distinguish the one scenario from the other.

One solution to this conundrum, which we call the average method, takes into consideration the number of valued lines, dividing the total value of lines to an actor by the number of lines. Thus, the average method calculates the mean value of the lines directly connected to an actor. This solution can distinguish between the two scenarios discussed in the preceding

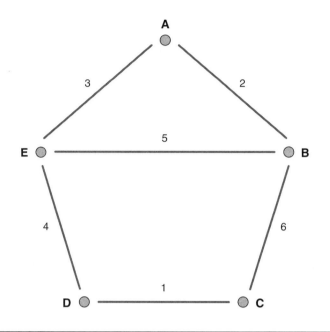

Figure 4.5 A Valued Nondirected Graph

paragraph. Suppose Actor X has five friends with low friendship values of 1, whereas Actor Y has only two friends but with higher values of 2 and 3. The summation method yields identical nodal valued degrees of 5 for both X and Y. The average method produces a mean of $\frac{1+1+1+1+1}{5} = 1$ for X and a mean of $\frac{2+3}{2} = 2.5$ for Y. Y's much higher average nodal degree shows that it has more intensive friendship ties than X.

Nodal degree measurement for valued directed graphs must take into account the directions of the relations by using indegrees or outdegrees. This table displays the results from applying the summation and average methods to the in- and outdegrees for the five nodes in Figure 4.6.

	Nodal Degrees	*A*	*B*	*C*	*D*	*E*
Summation Method	Indegrees	0	8	1	4	12
	Outdegrees	5	5	6	5	4
Average Method	Indegrees	0	4	1	4	4
	Outdegrees	2.5	5	6	2.5	4

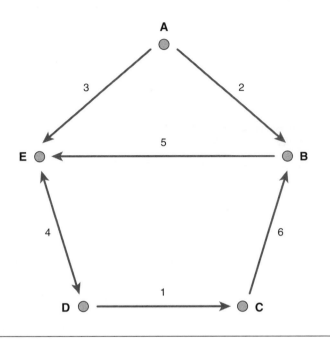

Figure 4.6   A Valued Directed Graph

A comparison of both methods yields some interesting findings. Using the average method, nodes B, D, and E have identical indegrees, indicating the equivalent popularity. In contrast, the summation method for indegrees reveals a steep hierarchy, with E very popular, followed by B, who is trailed by D. As shown in Figure 4.6, the summation method captures E as recipient of the most nominations with varying intensities, thus ranking E as the most popular. The average method stresses that although D received only one nomination, it has very high value, thus ranking D as popular as E and B. Depending on their research goals, network scholars may choose either method for measuring nodal degrees of valued directed graphs, being careful to interpret their results consistently with the ways those values are calculated.

Geodesic distance is the length of the shortest path between two actors. Its computation varies greatly across the four types of complete network data. Let's start with the simplest case: the binary nondirected graph in Figure 4.3. The nodes A and B are connected by many paths (e.g., AB, ACB, AEB, ADCB, ACDEB, AEDCB) with lengths from 1 to 4. The shortest path (AB) has path length 1, hence the geodesic distance between A and B is 1. Figure 4.3 contains 10 dyads ($C_5^2 = \frac{5!}{2! \times 3!} = 10$). The geodesic distances of these ten dyads vary depending on whether a dyad has direct connection. For example, geodesic distance of AB is 1, whereas geodesic distance for CE is 2 (via CDE, CBE, or CAE).

A directed graph with N actors has twice as many dyads as a nondirected graph of the same size, because each pair of actors has two ordered dyads in a directed graph rather than the single dyad of a nondirected graph. For example, the pair AB in Figure 4.4 has two dyads: AB and BA. A connects to B via two paths: AB and AEDCB (but AEB is not a path connecting A to B). The shortest path is AB, so the geodesic distance between AB is 1. Conversely, B is not connected to A, so the geodesic distance of dyad BA remains undefined. The geodesic distance analysis of directed graphs has many practical applications in network research. One common situation involves mapping of the communication routes among a set of actors. Suppose Figure 4.4 illustrates a communication network of five persons. Person A can send B messages either directly or indirectly via persons E, D, and C. But messages passing through intermediaries are vulnerable to delay and distortion, so A is most likely to communicate directly with B, as confirmed by the geodesic distance analysis of AB. In contrast, B cannot send messages to A either directly or indirectly. In fact, Person A can act only as a message sender, not as a message receiver, because nobody communicates with A. This example vividly illustrates that information flows may not be reciprocal.

Calculating geodesic distances in valued graphs encounters some difficulties in taking into consideration each path's values. We could reduce valued graphs into binary graphs, then apply the binary graph procedures, thereby wasting the rich information provided by the line values. Yang and Knoke (2001) proposed a solution using both the path length and the path values to measure geodesic distances of valued graph dyads. The method is implemented by a suitable algorithm (Yang & Hexmoor, 2004). In general, this solution involves (1) finding all paths connecting a dyad; (2) finding the lowest value of each path; (3) dividing the lowest value by the length of each path; and (4) choosing the highest value among the results of step 3, which is the geodesic distance of a valued graph (called *optimal connection* in Yang & Knoke, 2001). This method assumes that the long path length is the most costly in terms of delay and distortion and that the lowest path value identifies a bottleneck for dyadic interaction. The three paths connecting A with B in Figure 4.5, and their average path values, are AB $= 2$, AEB $= \frac{3}{2} = 1.5$, and AEDCB $= \frac{1}{4} = 0.25$. Choosing the highest average path value, the geodesic distance between A and B is 2, and thus the optimal path is AB.

Yang and Knoke's (2001) solution can be applied to calculating geodesic distances of dyads in valued directed graphs, except that the direction of the relations must be taken into consideration. The two paths connecting A to B in Figure 4.6 are AB, which has an average path value of 2, and AEDCB, which has an average path value of 0.25. Picking the largest path value, the geodesic distance connecting A to B is 2. However, the geodesic distance connecting B to A is undefined because B cannot reach A via any path.

Nodal degree and geodesic distance are important measures for social network analysis. Nodal degrees are easy to calculate, and often very informative in substantive applications. Nodal degree commonly indicates an actor's level of involvement in network activities. For example, a low nodal degree in a friendship network implies that person has few friends. For a complete network, the mean nodal degree shows the aggregate level of activity. For example, a low average nodal degree for community residents' visitations could reveal little neighboring activity. Nodal degree is also the basis for the degree centrality measure discussed in the next section. Geodesic distance between two nodes is the essential measure of their closeness. Because pairs of actors may be connected via several alternative paths, geodesic distance identifies the shortest path between each dyad and lays the foundations for aggregated, distance-based methods, such as multidimensional scaling and hierarchical clustering analyses discussed later in this chapter.

4.4. Centrality and Prestige

A primary use of graph theory in social network analysis is to identify the important or prominent actors at both the individual and group levels of analysis. Centrality and prestige concepts and measures seek to quantify graph theoretic ideas about an actor's prominence within a complete network by summarizing the structural relations among all nodes. Prominence takes into account both sociometric choices made and choices received, and sometimes also the structure of indirect ties. An individual actor's prominence reflects its greater visibility to the other network actors. Group-level indices of centralization and prestige assess the extent of a network's dispersion or inequality among all actor prominences. In this section we discuss two broad classes of prominence measures: (1) centrality, where a prominent actor has high involvement in many relations, regardless of whether sending or receiving ties; and (2) prestige, where a prominent actor initiates few relations but receives many directed ties. The choice among alternative prominence measures depends on both the conceptualization to be implemented and the types of social network data available. Their computations require applications of the matrix algebra notation discussed in a preceding section. Starting with the simplest case, we first discuss non-directed graphs, then digraphs. Because most prominence indicators require only binary tie measurement, our discussion is limited to such data, but we encourage network scholars to devote more effort to creating prominence measures for valued graphs.

The most widely used centrality measures are degree, closeness, and betweenness (Freeman, 1977, 1979). These measures vary in their applicability to nondirected and directed relations, and differ at the individual actor and the group or complete network levels. The computation formulas presented below use the notation of Wasserman and Faust (1994).

Degree Centrality. In a nondirected binary graph, *actor degree centrality* measures the extent to which a node connects to all other nodes in a social network. For a nondirected graph with g actors, the degree centrality for actor i is the sum of i's direct ties to the $g - 1$ other actors. In matrix notation,

$$C_D(N_i) = \sum_{j=1}^{g} x_{ij} (i \neq j) \tag{4.1}$$

where $C_D(N_i)$ denotes degree centrality for node i and $\sum_{j=1}^{g} x_{ij}$ counts the number of direct ties that node i has to the $g-1$ other j nodes ($i \neq j$ excludes i's relation to itself; i.e., the main diagonal values are ignored). The computation of $C_D(N_i)$ involves simply adding all the cell entries in either actor i's row or its column of a sociomatrix (because nondirected relations have a symmetric data matrix, the corresponding row and column cell entries must be identical).

Actor degree centrality so measured not only reflects each node's connectivity to other nodes but also depends on g, the size of the network; that is, the larger the network, the higher the maximum possible degree centrality value. Therefore, a particular degree centrality score could mean either that an actor is well connected within a small network, or that it is only connected to just a few others within a large network. To eliminate the effect of variation in network size on degree centrality, Wasserman and Faust (1994, p. 179) recommended a standardized measure:

$$C'_D(N_i) = \frac{C_D(N_i)}{g - 1} \tag{4.2}$$

This *normalized actor degree centrality* measure divides actor i's degree centrality score by the maximum number of possible connections with the $g - 1$ other actors, yielding the proportion of the network members with direct ties to actor i. Proportions vary between 0.0, indicating no connections with any actors (i.e., an isolate), and 1.0, reflecting direct ties to everyone. Normalized actor degree centrality measures the extent to which an actor is involved in numerous relationships. Actors with high scores are the most visible participants in a network. In particular, the closer the normalized degree centrality value approaches to 1.00, the greater the actor's involvement in a relational network. Researchers can readily apply this conceptualization of centrality in analyses of access, control, and brokerage in information networks, if they consider the sheer volume of activity to be more important than the specific sources and objects of nondirected relations (Knoke & Burt, 1983).

Unlike actor degree centrality, *group degree centralization* measures the extent to which the actors in a social network differ from one another in their individual degree centralities. Group degree centralization closely resembles measures of dispersion in descriptive statistics, such as the standard deviation, that indicate the amount of variation or spread around a central tendency value. Freeman (1979) proposed a generic measure of group degree centralization:

$$C_A = \frac{\sum\limits_{i=1}^{g} [C_A(N^*) - C_A(N_i)]}{\max \sum\limits_{i=1}^{g} [C_A(N^*) - C_A(N_i)]} \tag{4.3}$$

where $C_A(N^*)$ denotes the largest actor degree centrality observed in a network, and the $C_A(N_i)$ are the degree centralities of the $g-1$ other actors. Thus, the numerator sums the observed differences between the largest actor centrality and all the others. The denominator is the theoretically maximum possible sum of those differences.

Following Freeman's generic measure, Wasserman and Faust (1994, p. 180) proposed a procedure for the denominator in their *index of group degree centralization*:

$$C_D = \frac{\sum\limits_{i=1}^{g} [C_D(N^*) - C_D(N_i)]}{(g-1)(g-2)} \tag{4.4}$$

The numerator sums the observed differences in degree centralities between actor with the largest centrality and the other nodes. The denominator measures the maximum possible sum of differences. This value would occur in a *star graph*, where one node interacts with all the other nodes, but the others are tied only to the first node. The first node has the highest possible degree centrality $= (g - 1)$, whereas the other nodes each have degree centrality $= 1$; hence, the difference in centralities between this most central and any other node is $(g - 1) - 1 = g - 2$. Because this difference occurs $(g - 1)$ times in the graph, the value of the denominator is $(g - 1)(g - 2)$. The index of group degree centralization may take values between 0.0 and 1.0. When degree centrality in a social network is evenly dispersed, such that every node has the same degree centrality, $\sum_{i=1}^{g} [C_D(N^*) - C_D(N_i)]$ will be 0; thus, group degree centralization is 0. At the other extreme, degree centrality has maximum uneven dispersion when one node has the highest possible centrality $(g - 1)$ and all other nodes have degree centrality 1. The numerator then equals the denominator, and the index of group degree centralization equals 1.0. Therefore, the closer that group degree centralization is to 1.0, the more uneven or hierarchical is the degree centrality of nodes in a social network.

Closeness Centrality. *Actor closeness centrality* was developed to reflect how near a node is to the other nodes in a social network (Sabidussi, 1966). Closeness and distance refer to how quickly an actor can interact with others, for example, by communicating directly or through very few intermediaries. An actor's closeness centrality is a function of its geodesic distance to all other nodes (as defined above, geodesic distance is the length of the shortest path connecting a dyad). The *index of actor closeness centrality* is computed as the inverse of the sum of the geodesic distances between actor i and the $g - 1$ other actors:

$$C_C(N_i) = \frac{1}{\left[\sum_{j=1}^{g} d(N_i, N_j)\right]} (i \neq j) \tag{4.5}$$

This measure can never be 0.0 because division by zero is mathematically undefined. Thus, closeness centrality scores cannot be computed for isolated nodes (whose distances from i are undefined) and the index applies only to the nodes that form a connected graph. For empirical social network analysis, this restriction requires that every actor have a tie to at least one other member of the connected graph. The lowest actor closeness centrality values, and thus the high sum of the distances between a focal actor and others, result either from an actor in a relatively large network or an actor in a small network with relatively long distances from others.

When an actor is close to all others (i.e., has a direct tie to everyone in the network), $C_C = 1/(g - 1)$, which varies with network size. To control for

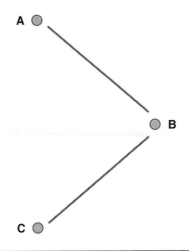

Figure 4.7   A Three-Node Nondirected Network

the size of the network, thus allowing meaningful comparisons of actors across different networks, Beauchamp (1965) recommended standardizing the index of actor closeness centrality by multiplying by $(g-1)$:

$$C'_C(N_i) = (g-1)(C_C(N_i)) \qquad (4.6)$$

To compare and contrast the closeness centrality and the normalized closeness centrality indices, we refer to two illustrations. Figure 4.7 shows a three-node network structure, in which Actor A is directly connected to B with geodesic distance of 1 and indirectly connected to C with geodesic distance of 2. Thus, the closeness centrality for A in Figure 4.7 is $1/(1+2) = 1/3$.

Figure 4.8 shows a four-node structure with direct connections between all nodes. Actor A has direct connection with Actors B, C, and D with geodesic distances of 1. Therefore, Actor A has a closeness centrality of $1/(1+1+1) = 1/3$. Although Actor A in Figure 4.8 has more direct ties to others than Actor A in Figure 4.7, both closeness indices are identical simply because the second network is larger. In contrast, the normalized closeness centrality distinguishes these two situations by taking network size into account. The normalized closeness centrality for Actor A in Figure 4.7 is $(3-1)(1/3) = 0.67$, whereas Actor A in Figure 4.8 has a higher value, $(4-1)(1/3) = 1.0$. The higher an actor's closeness centrality score, the closer it is to the other actors, in the sense that the actor can reach all others' nodes via shorter geodesic distances.

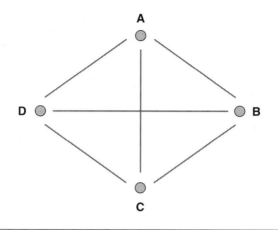

Figure 4.8   A Four-Node Completely Connected Network

Similar to group degree centralization, *group closeness centralization* is a dispersion measure indicating the hierarchy of closeness centralities within a network. Specifically, group closeness centralization measures the extent to which actors in a given network differ in their closeness centralities. Following Freeman (1979), an *index of group closeness centralization* is computed as

$$C_C = \frac{\sum_{i=1}^{g} [C'_C(N^*) - C'_C(N_i)]}{[(g-2)(g-1)]/(2g-3)} \tag{4.7}$$

where $C'_C(N^*)$ denotes the largest actor closeness centrality observed in a network, and the $C'_C(N_i)$ are the closeness centralities of the $g-1$ other actors. The group closeness centralization attains a maximum 1.0 when the network embraces a completely uneven distribution of actor closeness centralities, if one actor has the maximum closeness centrality and all others have the minimum closeness centralities. In contrast, group closeness centralization equals 0 when every actor has the same closeness centrality score.

Betweenness Centrality. The betweenness concept of centrality concerns how other actors control or mediate the relations between dyads that are not directly connected. *Actor betweenness centrality* measures the extent to which other actors lie on the geodesic path (shortest distance) between pairs of actors in the network. Betweenness centrality is an important indicator of control over information exchange or resource flows within a network. Suppose that actor j has to go through actor i to communicate with actor k. Actor i has responsibility or control over the content and timing in transmitting messages between actors j and k. The more often that actor i is located on the geodesic path between numerous dyads, the higher actor i's potential to control network interactions.

To quantify actor i's betweenness centrality, Freeman (1977) proposed the following procedure. First, g_{jk} is the number of geodesic paths between the two nodes j and k, and $g_{jk}(N_i)$ is the number of geodesics between the j and k that contain node i. Then, dividing $g_{jk}(N_i)$ by g_{jk} measures the proportion of geodesic paths connecting j and k in which node i is involved. Summing across all the dyads not including node i measures the extent to which i sits on the geodesic paths of the other network members. The following formula reflects this logic:

$$C_B(N_i) = \sum_{j < k} \frac{g_{jk}(N_i)}{g_{jk}} \qquad (4.8)$$

This index is 0.0 when node i falls on no geodesic path for all the pairs among the other $g - 1$ nodes. It reaches the maximum value of $(g - 1)$ $(g - 2)/2$ when node i falls on every geodesic path for all dyads, assuming that each pair has only one geodesic path. (Excluding node i, the total number of geodesic paths among the $g - 1$ nodes is $C_{g-1}^2 = \frac{(g-1)!}{2!(g-1-2)!} = \frac{(g-1)!}{2!(g-3)!} = \frac{(g-1)(g-2)}{2}$. However, if a dyad has more than one geodesic (shortest path), the maximum possible value for node i's betweenness centrality will be larger than $\frac{(g-1)(g-2)}{2}$, varying with the number of geodesic paths between each pair.

Wasserman and Faust (1994, p. 190) recommended standardizing actor betweenness centrality $C_B(n_i)$ by dividing by the maximum theoretical value of $\frac{(g-1)(g-2)}{2}$ (again, assuming that each pair has only one geodesic):

$$C_B'(N_i) = \frac{C_B(N_i) \times 2}{(g-1)(g-2)} \qquad (4.9)$$

The standardized actor betweenness centrality is 0.0 when the original betweenness centrality is 0, and it is 1.0 when node i falls on the geodesic paths of every dyad among the remaining $g - 1$ nodes. Therefore, the closer the standardized actor betweenness centrality is to 1.0, the more actor i controls or mediates relations in the network.

Like the group degree and closeness centralization measures, *group-level betweenness centralization* measures the extent to which this value varies across actors in a network. Following Freeman's (1979) generic method, Wasserman and Faust (1994) proposed this *index of group betweenness centralization*:

$$C_B = \frac{\sum_{i=1}^{g} [C_B(N^*) - C_B(N_i)]}{((g-1)^2(g-2))/2} \tag{4.10}$$

The numerator sums the differences in betweenness centrality scores for the actor with the highest value and every other actor. The denominator indicates the theoretically maximum possible value of betweenness centralities for all nodes in a network. Actor betweenness centrality attains its theoretical maximum at $\frac{(g-1)(g-2)}{2}$. At the group level, this maximum occurs, at most, $g-1$ times, if a single dominant node mediates all the others' geodesics. Thus, the theoretical maximum betweenness centralization for a network with g actors is $\frac{(g-1)^2(g-2)}{2}$. (Again, we stress that this computation assumes that each dyadic pair has only one geodesic path. If multiple geodesic paths occur for a dyad, the maximum possible actor betweenness centrality will be larger than $\frac{(g-1)(g-2)}{2}$, which produces a corresponding change in theoretical maximum possible value.)

Group betweenness centralization reaches 1.0 when a single dominant actor sits on all geodesic paths. In contrast, in a network where every node has the same betweenness centrality, the numerator is zero, and the group level centralization is 0.0. Thus, the closer the betweenness centralization approaches to 1.0, the more unequally distributed is betweenness centrality within the network.

Prestige. On many occasions, social network data collection involves instructions to specify the initiators or senders and the terminators or receivers of relations in a network. In such directed graphs, the mere participation or involvement in certain relations is less important than distinguishing senders and receivers. For example, in a reporting network of a workplace, lower-echelon employees routinely report to their managerial supervisors about their work activities and merit pay contributions, whereas higher-level employees rarely or never report their work activities to their subordinates. In a friendship network, a person enthusiastically nominating many others as her best friends may receive no best-friend nominations in return.

We define prestige as the extent to which a social actor in a network "receives" or "serves as the object" of relations sent by others in the network. The sender-receiver or source-target distinction strongly emphasizes inequalities in control over resources, as well as authority and deference accompanying such inequalities (Knoke & Burt, 1983, p. 199). In conformity to this definition, prestige can be measured simply by counting the number of directed ties that an actor receives from the other network actors for a specified relation. For example, Laumann and Knoke (1987, p. 163) asked informants in the U.S. energy and health policy domains to check the names of organizations on a list "that are *especially* influential and consequential in formulating national energy [health] policy." By treating each nomination as equal to another, without differentiating among the sources, the total nominations received reflects an actor's "popularity" within the system. Wasserman and Faust (1994, p. 202) proposed that *actor degree prestige* be calculated as the indegrees of a digraph:

$$P_D(N_i) = \sum_{j=1}^{g} x_{ji} \quad (j \neq i) \tag{4.11}$$

Because this measure sums the values in the ith column of an asymmetric sociomatrix of g nodes, its minimum value is 0.0 and maximum value is $g - 1$. A standardized actor degree prestige, by controlling for network size, allows prestige comparisons across different networks:

$$P'_D(N_i) = \frac{\sum_{j=1}^{g} x_{ji}}{g - 1} \quad (j \neq i) \tag{4.12}$$

Standardized prestige reaches 1.0 when all the other actors nominate actor i, but 0.0 if no one nominates actor i. Thus, the closer the proportion is to 1.0, the higher an actor's prestige.

The basic measures of centrality, centralization, and prestige described in the foregoing paragraphs are largely based on binary data. Studies of those corresponding measures on valued graphs are scarce, with the exception of Freeman, Borgatti, and White's (1991) discussion of betweenness centrality in valued graphs. Clearly, more research is needed to develop centrality and prestige measures applicable to valued graphs.

Centrality in Egocentric Networks. Analyses of centrality and prestige were limited to complete network data until Marsden (2002) extended centrality measures to egocentric data. He discussed centrality measures for binary symmetric data on a single relation. In egocentric research using survey respondents, egos nominate g alters with whom they have a specific relation. Each ego i generates a $(g+1) \times (g+1)$ data matrix, $\mathbf{A}_i$, whose rows and columns both consist of alters 1 through g plus ego i. Because ego by definition has direct ties with all of its alters, every element of the ith row is $x_{i,j} = 1$, where $1 \leq j \leq g$ and $i \neq j$.

Actor degree centrality in a complete network is the actor's direct connections to others (see equation 4.1). In an egocentric network with g alters, ego i's degree centrality is the maximum possible value of actor degree centrality, $g - 1$. The standardized degree centrality for ego i is always $\frac{g-1}{g-1} = 1.0$. Actor closeness centrality in a complete network is the inverse of the sum of geodesic distances between the actor i and others (see equation 4.5). The normalized closeness centrality controls for network size (see equation 4.6). Thus, ego's closeness centrality and normalized closeness centrality are $\frac{1}{g-1}$ and $\frac{g-1}{g-1} = 1.0$, respectively. Finally, betweenness centrality in a complete network measures the extent to which node i sits on the geodesic distances of all pairs (see equation 4.8). Because ego i is directly connected to all alters in its own egocentric network, i serves as intermediary for each alter dyad that is not directly connected.

Marsden (2002, p. 410) asserted that betweenness centrality for node i in an egocentric network differs from that measure applied to a complete network. On one hand, the betweenness centrality for node i can be biased downwardly in egocentric data. The egocentric betweenness measure does not include the ego node i's intermediary location between any pair of nodes connected via geodesic distances with path lengths of three or more, but that situation is included in the complete network betweenness measure. On the other hand, egocentric betweenness centrality can exaggerate ego node i's betweenness centrality if two alters are connected both through i and also through another node lying outside i's egocentric network. In this case, the intermediary node outside the egocentric network is ignored in the egocentric betweenness measure but is included in the complete betweenness centrality measure.

To illustrate these points, examine Figure 4.9. The egocentric network of actor ego i consists of four alters, A, B, C, and D, nominated on some relation. The complete network also includes node M, which is connected to two of i's alters (A and D) although M itself isn't part of i's egocentric network. The four alters of i have six dyads (AB, AC, AD, BC, BD, and CD), each with one unique geodesic path. Because only the BC dyad is directly connected, while the geodesic paths connecting the remaining pairs of alters all include ego i, i's betweenness centrality in its egocentric network is 5/6. However, the presence of node M generates differences in the egocentric- and complete-network betweenness centralities of i. On one hand, the egocentric betweenness measure of i is biased downward by overlooking the intermediary locations of i on two geodesic paths (for dyads MB and MC). On the other hand, the egocentric betweenness of i is biased upward by omitting the geodesic for AD through M, which competes with the AD geodesic through i.

Despite such divergences between the egocentric and complete network betweenness measures, Marsden (2002) demonstrated that both measures

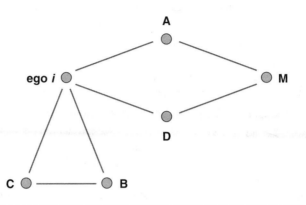

Figure 4.9   Betweenness Centrality in an Egocentric Network

closely correspond to one another in his analyses of 17 empirical networks. Therefore, egocentric betweenness centrality appears to be a reliable substitute for actor betweenness centrality in a complete network when the latter is difficult to obtain. Marsden (2002) argued that the data collection differences between egocentric and complete networks may account for the divergences between the two betweenness results, pinpointing an important topic deserving further systematic investigation.

4.5. Cliques

Cohesion is closely related to ideas of dense, intimate relations among members embedded in a social group or closed social circle. A *cohesive subgroup* consists of actors connected through many direct, reciprocated choice relations that enable them to share information, create solidarity, and act collectively. Numerous direct contacts among all subgroup members, combined with few or no ties to outsiders, dispose a group toward homogeneity of thought, identity, and behavior. Examples of cohesive groups include religious cults, terrorist cells, criminal gangs, military platoons, sports teams, craft occupations, and work teams. The term clique ("kleek" or "klick") has passed into everyday language, referring to the high-status in-crowds of schools, churches, and clubs. The concept has acquired specificity in network analysis, derived from such graph theoretic elements as node, line, and path distance. Using clique analysis to investigate group structures helps researchers understand better how cohesion benefits group members by providing advice and instrumental support

(Dunbar & Spoor, 1995), and how an extensive reliance on cliques restricts the range of network contacts (Blau, Ruan, & Ardelt, 1991).

Often sociological concepts such as group, cluster, circle, gang, faction, and clique are used interchangeably without rigorous distinctions (Borgatti, Everett, & Shirey, 1990). Summarizing the vast literature on subgroups in social network studies, Wasserman and Faust (1994, p. 251) extracted four general properties that characterize cohesive subgroups: mutuality of ties, reachability of subgroup members, frequency of ties among members, and relative frequency of ties among subgroup members compared with non-members. These characteristics lay the foundation for operationally defining cliques and related measures of network subgroups.

Cliques. A *clique* is a maximal complete subgraph of three or more nodes, all of which are directly connected to one another, with no other node in the network having direct ties to every member of the clique. Hence, the geodesic distance for every pair of nodes in a clique is 1.0; that is, each dyad is connected by a direct path. Figure 4.10 illustrates cliques in a binary nondirected network of six nodes. Two cliques (ABE and BCDE) each meet the necessary requirements. Although F has ties to both A and C, these three nodes do not make up a clique because A and C are not directly connected. Four other small groupings (EBC, EBD, BCD, and BDE) are also not cliques because one additional node is directly connected to all three nodes in these groupings. For example, EBC is not a clique because node D has direct ties to E, B, and C. Only the maximal complete subgraph BCDE qualifies as a clique.

As a method for identifying cohesive subgroups, the clique criteria impose very strict conditions. The clique concept has earned a reputation as "stingy" (Alba, 1973) because the absence of just a single line may prevent a subgraph from being a clique. Given this high threshold for clique formation, empirical researchers rarely detect large cliques in low-density real networks (Wasserman & Faust 1994, p. 256). One reason for the scarcity of cliques in actual network data lies in the design of network data collection. For example, the fixed list approach may restrict respondents to nominating a specified maximum number of alters ("name your three best friends"). Thus, clique size cannot exceed any ceiling imposed by researchers.

The clique criteria also rigorously separate members inside a cohesive subgroup from everyone outside, thus overlooking gradations between the more central and more peripheral actors. Once a clique boundary is drawn, no finer distinctions can be made between clique and nonclique members. Such simple dichotomization often is not very informative because it fails to reflect more important but subtle distinctions. One determinant of the number of cliques in a graph is the size of the complete network. Small networks rarely yield any cliques, whereas large datasets often proliferate

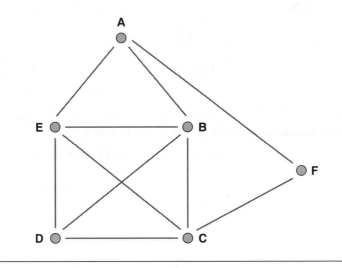

Figure 4.10   Cliques in a Nondirected Graph

numerous tiny cliques, many of which overlap with one another. This limitation led researchers to focus on multiple overlapping cliques rather than searching for a single, stand-alone clique.

***n*-cliques.** Although the rigid clique definition prevents it from being very informative, it catalyzed subsequent measures of subgroup cohesion that relax the stringent requirements for clique detection. One general approach is based on nodal degree, the number of lines incident on a node (Doreian & Woodard, 1994; Seidman,1983). We discussed this approach in Chapter 3 under the *k-core* concept, which defines a subgroup as a *k-core* if every member has direct ties to at least *k* other nodes. By changing the value of *k*, a researcher can set more or less restrictive criteria for bounding a subgroup.

A second general approach modifies the clique using nodal connectivity (Alba, 1973; Mokken, 1979). The *n-clique* concept relaxes the rigid clique requirement that the geodesic distances between every dyad must be 1.0. In *n*-cliques, the maximum geodesic distance between all pairs is path length *n*; that is, no node can be more than *n* links away from every other node. By varying the value of *n*, network researchers can differentiate subgroups with greater cohesiveness (small *n*) or lower cohesiveness (large *n*). For example, setting *n* equal to 2 identifies a 2-clique as a subset of three or more nodes, all of whose geodesics are 2 or less, while all other nodes in the network are connected to the 2-clique with geodesic distances of 3 or more. In the nondirected graph in Figure 4.10, node F did not belong to either clique

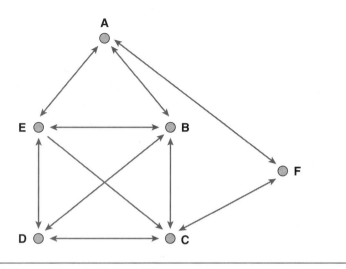

Figure 4.11   Cliques in a Directed Graph

under the stringent criteria. However, relaxing the geodesic distance from 1 to 2 identifies a 2-clique (the entire graph, ABCDEF) that includes F, because it (as well as A) is connected to all the 2-clique members with geodesic distances of 2 or less. The *n*-clique criterion specifies that the maximum geodesic distance between any dyad cannot exceed *n*. In general, the larger the value of *n*, the more inclusive the *n*-clique, and therefore the less cohesion among its members, because some pairs will be as much as *n*-steps away from one another. The strict definition of a clique is a special case of an *n*-clique in which *n* equals 1.0.

Cliques in Digraphs. Directed graphs distinguish relational senders from receivers. Identifying cliques in directed graphs attends to the reciprocity of dyadic ties. To extend the strict definition of a clique used for nondirected graphs, a *digraph clique* is a subgraph with three or more nodes, all directly connected to one another, where each pair is reciprocally connected (i.e., mutual ties). To illustrate digraph clique detection, Figure 4.11 shows a network of directed ties among six nodes. Three triadic cliques are present (ABE, BDE, and BCD). Because the relation from E to C is not reciprocated, EBCD doesn't make up a digraph clique. Similarly, the absence of direct mutual ties between A and C prevents AFC from being a digraph clique.

Drawing on the *n*-clique definition for nondirected graphs, researchers proposed relaxing the rigid clique requirements by allowing varying geodesic distances between mutually connected digraph nodes. The approaches bear great similarity, except that more considerations apply to directed ties. For example, two nodes can be n-connected via four scenarios: weakly n-connected, unilaterally n-connected, strongly n-connected, and recursively n-connected (see Peay, 1980; Wasserman & Faust, 1994, p. 275). In the strongest form of n-connection—recursively n-connected—the shortest path (geodesic) from i to j and the shortest path from j to i must use the same nodes in reverse order and have a path length of n or less. Each of the four scenarios may define a digraph n-clique, producing four types of n-clique subgroups. In Figure 4.11, the subgraph ABCDF is recursively 2-connected because its ten dyads are mutually reachable by reverse geodesics of length 1 or 2. However, E cannot be included because its nonreversible tie to C makes this geodesic shorter than either of the two geodesics connecting C to E (C-D-E and C-B-E).

4.6. Structural Equivalence

Social scientists are often interested not only in actor cohesion but also in the equivalence of actors, in the sense of two or more actors having identical or very similar relations with others in a network. Structurally equivalent actors typically have a competitive, rather than a cohesive, relation. For example, two cabbage growers who market their produce to the same set of retailers are structurally equivalent and in stiff competition to sell their vegetables. Structurally equivalent actors are completely substitutable for one another. If one farmer were to withdraw from the food network, it could easily be replaced by a structurally equivalent farmer, leaving the original network structure unchanged. Perfect substitutability in a social network often generates fierce competition to obtain favorable responses from other network participants (as is well known to grade-schoolers competing for their teacher's attention). Network scholars who use structural equivalence methods are generally interested in understanding competitive relations rather than group cohesion (Burt, 1992).

Similar to clique identification, the definition of structural equivalence is very rigorous. In a directed binary graph, two actors are perfectly *structurally equivalent* in that specific relation if they have exactly identical patterns of ties sent to and received from all the other network actors. More precisely, nodes i and j are structurally equivalent if, for all nodes k in the network (but not including i or j), node i sends a tie to node k, if and only if j also sends a tie to k, and node i receives a tie from k if and only if j also receives a tie from k (Wasserman & Faust, 1994, p. 356). For multiple networks, this condition must hold precisely in each of the R relations for the two nodes to be structurally equivalent. The presence or absence of directed ties between nodes i and j is irrelevant to determining whether they are structurally equivalent. Rather, their structural equivalence is determined only by their patterns of relations with the $g - 2$ other network nodes.

Nondirected binary graphs make no distinction between senders and receivers of relations. Thus, extending the preceding definition of digraph structural equivalence to a nondirected graph, actors i and j are perfectly structurally equivalent if, for all other actors k, i has a tie with k if and only if j has a tie with k. Structural equivalence can also be applied to valued graphs, in which ranking scales rather than binary values measure the ties between nodes. Strictly speaking, two valued-graph nodes are perfectly structurally equivalent only when both have exactly identical values in every tie to all other nodes.

The preceding definitions of perfect structural equivalence are usually too rigorous for practical applications in empirical network analyses. Real network data rarely contain any dyads that meet such stringent standards. However, some nodes may be approximately structurally equivalent, in the sense that their patterns of relations with the other nodes are highly similar to one another although not identical. To capture such approximations, researchers use measures of relational similarity rather than applying a rigid, all-or-nothing requirement of perfect structural equivalence. The more similar two nodes are in their respective connections with all the other nodes, the greater is their structural equivalence.

Structural equivalence based on relational similarity for a network dyad only requires that their patterns of present and absent ties to and from the other actors be highly similar. Assuming a binary digraph, two structurally equivalent actors will have entries in the corresponding rows and columns of the sociomatrix that closely resemble one another. Operationalizing this criterion, Burt (1978) proposed Euclidean distance as a measure of the structural equivalence of actors i and j:

$$d_{ij} = \sqrt{\sum_{k=1}^{g} [(x_{ik} - x_{jk})^2 + (x_{ki} - x_{kj})^2]} \quad (i \neq j \neq k) \qquad (4.13)$$

where d_{ij} is the Euclidean distance between actors i and j, and the x's are the values (either 1 or 0 for binary relations) in the sociomatrix (the first subscript denotes the row and the second subscript the column). Because d_{ij} is the positive square root of the sum of two squared difference terms, every $d_{ij} \geq 0$. If actors i and j have exactly identical ties to all others, all the differences $(x_{ik} - x_{jk})$ and $(x_{ki} - x_{kj})$ are zero; therefore, two perfectly structurally equivalent actors have Euclidean distance $d_{ij} = 0$. But in most empirical cases, observed values of d_{ij} are greater than zero; hence, actors i and j are relationally similar to some varying extent. Euclidean distance is inverse to actor similarity and hence to structural equivalence: The larger the d_{ij}, the less the structural equivalence of actors i and j. In other words, Euclidean distances actually measure the dissimilarities between pairs of actors.

To illustrate how to compute Euclidean distances for a dyad, Figure 4.12 and Table 4.3 depict a five-node network structure in digraph and matrix forms, respectively. Figure 4.12 shows that Actors A and B are perfectly structurally equivalent because they both have direct connections to Actors C and D and no tie to Actor E. In contrast, Actors D and E are not structurally equivalent because, despite each sending a tie to Actor C, Actor D receives ties from Actors A and B, but Actor E receives no ties. Using the binary values from Table 4.3, the Euclidean distance between Actors A and B is the following:

$$d_{AB} = \sqrt{\begin{array}{c} [(x_{AC} - x_{BC})^2 + (x_{CA} - x_{CB})^2] + [(x_{AD} - x_{BD})^2 + \\ (x_{DA} - x_{DB})^2] + [(x_{AE} - x_{BE})^2 + (x_{EA} - x_{EB})^2] \end{array}}$$

$$d_{12} = \sqrt{\begin{array}{c} [(1 - 1)^2 + (0 - 0)^2] + [(1 - 1)^2 + (0 - 0)^2] + \\ [(0 - 0)^2 + (0 - 0)^2] \end{array}} \quad (4.14)$$

$d_{12} = 0$, indicating that actors A and B are perfectly structurally equivalent. *Can you show that the Euclidean distance between actors D and E is $\sqrt{2} = 1.41$?*

Because nondirected binary graphs make no distinction between senders and receivers of relations, computing Euclidean distance is simpler:

$$d_{ij} = \sqrt{\sum_{k=1}^{g} (x_{ik} - x_{jk})^2} \quad (i \neq j \neq k) \quad (4.15)$$

When multiple relations are present in the network, the Euclidean distance computation involves summing squared differences for a dyad across all R relations:

$$d_{ij} = \sqrt{\sum_{r=1}^{R} \sum_{k=1}^{g} [(x_{ikr} - x_{jkr})^2 + (x_{kir} - x_{kjr})^2]} \quad (i \neq j \neq k) \quad (4.16)$$

In contrast to Euclidean distance as a measure of dissimilarity, Pearson's correlation coefficient (r_{ij}) directly measures relational similarity, with higher values of dyadic correlation indicating greater structural

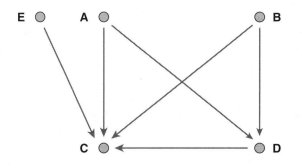

Figure 4.12   Digraph of a Five-Node Network for Structural Equivalence

TABLE 4.3
Matrix of a Five-Node Network for Structural Equivalence

	A	B	C	D	E
A	–	0	1	1	0
B	0	–	1	1	0
C	0	0	–	0	0
D	0	0	1	–	0
E	0	0	1	0	–

equivalence. We discuss correlations in the blockmodeling section later in this chapter.

4.7. Visual Displays

Images of networks are commonly created in social network studies to develop structural insights and to communicate those insights to others. Social network analysis experienced three distinctive periods of visual display innovation (Freeman, 2000, 2005). The initial stage began in the 1930s, when Jacob Moreno developed hand-drawn, ad hoc sociograms to depict relations among actors such as schoolchildren (Moreno, 1934). This freestyle approach gave way to standard computational procedures for plotting the points and lines of a graph. A basic principle from the initial era of visualization is that spatial representations should preserve the underlying pattern of actor ties, by depicting pairs that are socially closest in a data matrix as closest in a graphic image (Freeman, 2005). However, preserving precise proximities and distances among numerous actors in two- or three-dimensional visual displays is usually impossible, so researchers eventually developed methods for systematically simplifying and reducing the number of dimensions while still reflecting the original data patterns. The second phase of visualization, beginning around the 1960s, used mainframe computers and software to produce graphics automatically. In particular, network analysts made increasing use of the hierarchical clustering and multidimensional scaling methods described in this section. In the most recent phase, starting in the mid-1990s with the advent of the World Wide Web, high-speed computer networks and browsers, and widespread personal computers opened new opportunities for large-scale visual displays of relational data, including animation of longitudinal network changes (for example, Brandes, Kenis, Raab, Schneider, & Wagner, 1999; de Nooy, Mrvar, & Batagelj, 2005).

Lacking space to cover all these developments in depth, we concentrate on explicating the fundamental ideas of two tools, hierarchical clustering and multidimensional scaling, for displaying relations in network data. Visual displays are useful for exploring social network data to uncover cohesive subgroups and to reveal how they relate to one another. In this process, complex network structures can be simplified by reducing their representation from many actors to a smaller number of *jointly occupied positions*. Structural equivalence methods compute and analyze a matrix of dyadic dissimilarities (Euclidean distances) or similarities (correlation coefficients) to identify network positions that are jointly occupied by subgroups of actors with either identical or very similar patterns of ties to others. Clustering and multidimensional scaling methods applied to a matrix of structural equivalence measures identify jointly occupied positions, displaying the results as a two- or three-dimensional diagram.

Clustering. *Hierarchical agglomerative cluster analysis*, or cluster analysis for short, partitions actors into subgroups (jointly occupied positions) whose members are perfectly or approximately structurally equivalent. Each actor is treated initially as a singleton cluster, and then clusters are successively joined until all actors merge into a single remaining cluster. A *tree diagram*, also called a *dendrogram*, visually depicts this hierarchical sequence of merging clusters.

Clustering algorithms typically process a square $g \times g$ matrix of either Euclidean distances (d_{ij}) or correlation coefficients (r_{ij}), where g is the number of actors in a specific relation. One comparative study of cluster analyses suggested that both measures produce very similar results, although cluster analyses using correlations may be somewhat easier to interpret (Aldenderfer & Blashfield, 1984, pp. 24–28). Multiple network relations (R) can be clustered simultaneously by constructing a data array with dimensions $g \times g \times R$, then computing Euclidean distances or correlations for every dyad across all R matrices before conducting the cluster analysis. Although hierarchical agglomerative clustering can be performed on both binary and valued data, for simplicity we focus on symmetric binary matrices of Euclidean distances.

After computing a matrix of pairwise Euclidean distances, a cluster analysis proceeds to combine actors according to a threshold value, α, which serves as a ceiling, or upper bound, for the analyst to decide which actors belong in the same jointly occupied position (cluster) at a particular level of structural equivalence. Actors i and j jointly occupy a position only if $d_{ij} \leq \alpha$. Actors within one cluster have smaller social distances from one another (i.e., are more structurally equivalent) than from the actors occupying other clusters. The clustering algorithm proceeds incrementally, applying successively less-restrictive levels of α (i.e., higher values of α) to aggregate actors into positions, until the entire network merges into a single all-inclusive cluster. Although hierarchical agglomerative clustering produces nonoverlapping clusters, the clusters are nested; that is, smaller clusters are subsumed within successively larger clusters at higher values of α (i.e., lower structural equivalence, less similarity, greater within-cluster distances). Ultimately, the researcher must decide which level of agglomeration (i.e., which value of α) provides the best substantive representation of the number of structurally equivalent positions in the network.

Researchers may choose from among three basic criteria for forming clusters: single link, average link, or complete link. At a given level of α, the single-link criterion merges two clusters into one cluster when their two closest actors have distance less than α. Under complete link, two clusters merge when the distance between every pair of actors is less than α. The average linkage option is a compromise, requiring that two merging clusters have an average distance among both sets of actors that is less than α. Empirical analysts reported advantages and disadvantages from using each option, which should prompt researchers planning to use cluster analysis to be acutely attuned to those issues (Aldenderfer & Blashfield, 1984, pp. 53–62). Complete link clustering appears to produce large numbers of homogeneous and tightly bound clusters, with a lower probability of "chaining," the formation of a single large cluster by successively adding one actor at a time (Burgin, 1995; Wasserman & Faust, 1994, p. 381).

The preceding sections discussed closely related concepts and methods of cliques, clusters, and structural equivalence. Those network methods are commonly used to uncover the building blocks of social structure, such as the extent of social cohesiveness (cliques and clusters) or structural competition (structural equivalence). Because the methods examine the middle level of social structures, they link the micropatterns of social networks to the global network social structure. The next section discusses multidimensional scaling, another important method for uncovering underlying structures among network actors.

Multidimensional scaling. *Multidimensional scaling* (MDS) is a second basic method for visualizing data structures. The primary purpose of MDS is to detect meaningful underlying dimensions that reflect the similarities or dissimilarities (distances) among network actors. As in cluster analysis, the typical input to MDS is a $g \times g$ matrix of either Euclidean distances (d_{ij}) or correlation coefficients (r_{ij}), where g is the number of actors in a specific relation. An MDS visual output is a plot, or social map, in which actors with smaller distances (greater similarities) between them are located closer in space than are actors with larger distances (greater dissimilarities). Although the MDS diagrams can represent multiple dimensions, most analysts display two- or three-dimensional maps.

The distances between actors displayed in an MDS map are related to, but not identical to, the similarity or dissimilarity values in the input matrix. Rather, they reflect the pairwise distances estimated from those data by the MDS program. A *stress* indicator measures the discrepancies across all pairs between the observed matrix and the computed matrix (Kruskal & Wish, 1978, pp. 23–30):

$$Stress = \sqrt{\frac{\sum \sum (f(x_{ij}) - d_{ij})^2}{Scale}} \tag{4.17}$$

where $f(x_{ij})$ is a nonmetric, monotonic function of the input values (Kruskal & Wish, 1978, p. 29) and d_{ij} is the Euclidean distance between actors i and j as displayed in the map coordinates. *Scale* is a scaling factor that constrains the stress values between 0.0 and 1.0. If an MDS map perfectly reproduces the input data, then $f(x_{ij}) = d_{ij}$ for all i and j, and thus stress would equal zero. Hence, the lower the stress value, the more closely an MDS spatial diagram represents the observed social distances among the network actors. For this reason, stress is also dubbed a badness-of-fit measure of MDS, in that stress values below 0.1 are considered an excellent fit, values between 0.1 and 0.2 are an adequate fit, and values above 0.2 are a poor fit (Kruskal & Wish, 1978, p. 52; Slez & Martin, 2007).

MDS has been used to facilitate various studies. For example, Slez and Martin (2007) used MDS to map the states with regards to their voting similarity over time. White, Kim, and Glick (2005) mapped the sociospatial positions of 50 ethnic groups in Toronto. The biggest advantage of MDS was in allowing them to analyze all ethnic groups simultaneously, in

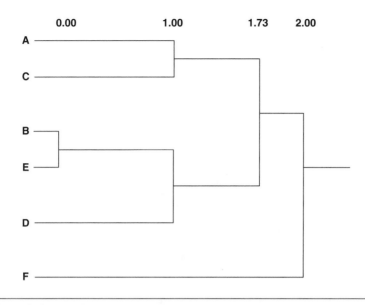

Figure 4.13   Hierarchical Dendrogram of Network in Figure 4.12

contrast to conventional approaches to segregation that analyze one group versus all others.

To illustrate how the two methods of clustering and MDS can work together to reveal structurally equivalent network positions, both the hierarchical cluster dendrogram in Figure 4.13 and the MDS map in Figure 4.14 are based on Euclidean distances computed from the binary network data represented in Figure 4.12. The cluster analysis uses the complete link option: Clusters merge when the distance among all their actors was less than α (these values appear on the horizontal axis of Figure 4.13). For example, the Euclidean distance (α) between Actors B and E is 0.00 (a complete structural equivalence), so that the dendrogram merges B and E first at Euclidean distance $= 0.00$. Two clusters appear at Euclidean distance $= 1.00$: One cluster combines Actors A and C, and the other merges D into the existing B-E cluster. At $\alpha = 1.73$, both clusters merge, indicating that the Euclidean distance between all dyads is less than 1.73. Finally, Actor F merges with the A-B-C-D-E cluster at the Euclidean distance $= 2.00$, showing that the Euclidean distance between F and the other actors lies between 1.73 and 2.00.

The MDS map in Figure 4.14 has contiguity lines around subgroups of actors jointly occupying the three clusters identified when the $\alpha = 1.00$

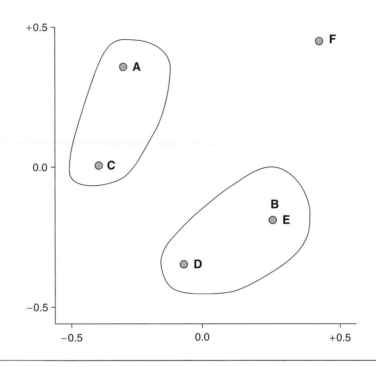

Figure 4.14   Multidimensional Scaling of Network in Figure 4.12

in the clustering dendogram. Actors B and E occupy exactly the same point in the map because they are perfectly structurally equivalent. Although a choice of α for identifying clusters is somewhat arbitrary, we recommend choosing a value that balances between cohesion and divisiveness among network actors. For example, had we chosen Euclidean distance of 0.00, we would have five clusters: B and E forming one cluster and the other four actors each occupying singleton clusters. In contrast, had we chosen $\alpha = 2.00$, only two clusters would result—(A-B-C-D-E) and (F). The first criterion yields tremendous divisiveness due to the high threshold for "being close," whereas the second value would produce great cohesiveness due to the low threshold. Neither approach seems as informative as a middling $\alpha = 1.00$, revealing structural relations among jointly occupied positions that strike a more balanced view of this network's divisions and cohesion.

An extension is weighted multidimensional scaling (WMDS), which adds a component (weight) to the conventional MDS approach, to represent information about variation between matrices. Thus, WMDS generalizes the distance model by allowing multiple matrices to be systematically differentiated. For example, if each matrix corresponds to a different individual, WMDS uses the weight to portray differences in how those individuals think about or perceive relations. For this reason, WMDS is also called individual differences scaling (INDSCAL). Although we cannot elaborate here on WMDS, we encourage interested readers to consult Schiffman, Reynolds, and Young (1981, pp. 55–85) and a recent application by Han (2003).

4.8. Blockmodels

Blockmodeling is a matrix algebraic method for sorting network actors into jointly occupied, structurally equivalent positions. Blockmodel methods were initially developed by Harrison White and his associates (Boorman & White, 1976; Schwartz, 1977; White et al., 1976). Since that groundbreaking work, researchers have fruitfully applied blockmodeling methods to various topics ranging from interorganizational networks (Knoke & Rogers, 1979), to diffusion of new technology (Anderson & Jay, 1985), to the roles of cities in the world system (Alderson & Beckfield, 2004). Methodological researchers also extended the blockmodel searching and partitioning algorithms (Nowicki & Snijders, 2001; Winship & Mandel, 1983; Wu, 1983). Because space limitation prohibits an extended discussion on this large literature, we focus on fundamental issues of blockmodeling methods, implementation, and interpretation of outputs.

A *blockmodel* is the partition of a sociomatrix of g actors, in one or more relational networks, into two or more discrete subgroups or positions, called *blocks* (B). The term *block* refers to a square submatrix of structurally equivalent actors that have very similar, if not identical, relations with the actors occupying the other blocks. Blockmodeling is a data reduction technique that systematically searches for relational patterns in network data by regrouping actors and presenting condensed aggregate-level information. The outputs are permuted density and image matrices displaying the pattern of ties within and between the blocks for each type of relation. Blockmodeling can be applied to single or multiple relations, directed or nondirected ties, and binary or valued graphs. Our blockmodel examples are based on UCINET's CONCOR algorithm, which can handle both binary and valued graphs. We examine only binary matrices and refer readers to an elaborated discussion of blockmodeling for both binary and valued graphs by Doreian, Batagelj, and Ferligoj (2005, pp. 347–360).

A blockmodel could be constructed a priori using theoretical principles, for example, by sorting the employees of different bureaucratic departments into separate blocks. However, the most common applications of the method are exploratory searches for empirical patterns in a relational dataset. Blockmodeling is often implemented using CONCOR (**Con**vergence of iterated **Cor**relations), which is available in several social network analysis programs (Schwartz, 1977). CONCOR can operate by correlating pairs of rows, pairs of columns, or both matrix vectors simultaneously. For didactic simplicity, we correlate only the columns. In its initial step, CONCOR calculates Pearson correlation coefficients for every pair of columns in a binary $g \times g$ sociomatrix. (To blockmodel R multiple relations, the separate $g \times g$ matrices are "stacked" [arranged as a single two-dimensional data array] for input to CONCOR.) These computations exclude the direct ties between each dyad, as their structural equivalence depends only on the pair's ties to the other $g - 2$ network actors. If actors i and j have exactly identical connections with all other actors, their correlation coefficient, r_{ij}, will equal 1.0. In contrast, if two actors have exactly opposite patterns of connections, their correlation will be -1.0. Almost always, empirical correlation coefficients fall somewhere between these extreme values. The result from the initial CONCOR step is a symmetric $g \times g$ matrix of correlations for every pair of actors, showing the extent of each dyad's structural equivalence. The second step, and all subsequent iterations, repeats this process of correlating pairs of columns in the correlation matrix produced by the preceding step. At some point, the correlation coefficients in every cell converge to either 1.0 or -1.0, at which point the iterations cease.

Next, CONCOR permutes the final correlation matrix into two homogeneous blocks. *Permutation* of a sociomatrix involves simultaneously rearranging both the rows and columns to bring together in adjacent portions those actors jointly occupying the same block. CONCOR's initial partition and permutation of the sociomatrix always yields two submatrices, not necessarily having equal numbers of actors, in which all the correlation coefficients among pairs of actors within each block equal 1.0, but all the correlations between the two blocks equal -1.0. Repeating these procedures, CONCOR can subdivide each of the two initial blocks into two more blocks, and so on. The network researcher must decide where to stop the division process, thus determining the ultimate number of blocks obtained.

Blockmodel analysis results in two primary forms of output: a density matrix and a corresponding image matrix. A *density matrix* is a $b \times b$ matrix whose cell values are the densities within and between the blocks. (Density is a proportion calculated by dividing the number of observed ties in a permuted submatrix by the number of possible ties.) An *image matrix* is also a $b \times b$ matrix, obtained from the density matrix by recoding each cell density to either 0 or 1. Two alternative criteria may be used to determine the image values: (1) any cell with no ties among its actors (*zero-block*) is recoded as 0, and any cell with at least one tie among its members (*one-block*) is recoded as 1; or (2) the researcher chooses a *density cutoff*, alpha (α), recoding all densities below this cutoff to 0, and all proportions of α or higher to 1. The first option is an unrealistic standard, because empirical densities of 0.0 seldom occur unless a network has very few relations, so almost all image matrices would consist only of 1s in every cell. The second option, using an alpha density cutoff to dichotomize the image values, is the most common practice. Researchers typically choose the density of the full matrix as the cutoff value. However, because choosing an alpha value inevitably involves the researcher's judgment, selecting a particular value is vulnerable to the criticism of arbitrariness. In response, researchers should try to justify their choices on theoretical and empirical grounds, rather than appealing solely to expediency (Scott, 1991, p. 136).

As a substantive application of blockmodeling, we analyze the policy communication network of the U.S. national labor policy domain in 1988, when the Reagan Administration controlled the executive branch (Knoke et al., 1996). The core consists of the 24 reputedly most influential political organizations, as identified by a checklist filled out by informants from the larger set of 117 domain organizations (see Table 4.4 for the key to organizational acronyms). Figure 4.15 is the digraph of confirmed communication about labor policy matters (for a directed tie to exist, a pair of organizations must agree that information sent was also received). The high density of ties within this core (0.29) renders any simple structure in this graph difficult to discern. The corresponding communication matrix, in Table 4.4, was transformed into a matrix of correlations using both rows (senders) and columns (receivers). These correlations measure relational similarities in each pair of organizations' communication patterns with the other 22 core domain organizations. The correlation matrix was then subjected to a CONCOR analysis, producing the four-block partition, density, and image matrices in Table 4.6.

For determining the 1-blocks in the image, a density cutoff (α) of 0.33 or higher was used. Finally, in Figure 4.16, the MDS analysis of the correlation matrix shows the distances among the core organizations, with contiguity lines enclosing the members of the four blocks.

TABLE 4.4

Binary Matrix of Core Communication Network
in U.S. Labor Policy Domain

		1	2	3	4	5	6	7	8	9	1 0	1 1	1 2	1 3	1 4	1 5	1 6	1 7	1 8	1 9	2 0	2 1	2 2	2 3	2 4
1	AFL	0	1	1	1	1	0	0	1	1	0	0	0	0	0	1	1	1	1	0	0	1	1	1	1
2	ASCM	1	0	0	1	0	0	0	0	0	0	0	1	0	0	1	0	0	0	0	0	0	0	1	0	0
3	TEAM	0	0	0	1	0	0	1	0	1	0	0	0	1	0	0	0	0	1	1	1	1	1	1	0
4	UAW	1	0	1	0	1	0	0	0	0	0	0	0	0	0	0	0	0	0	0	0	0	1	0	1
5	USW	1	0	0	1	0	0	0	1	0	0	0	0	0	0	0	0	0	0	0	0	1	1	0	0
6	ABC	0	0	0	0	0	0	1	1	1	0	1	0	0	0	0	1	0	1	0	1	1	1	1	0
7	AGC	0	0	1	0	0	1	0	1	1	0	1	0	0	0	0	1	0	1	0	1	1	1	1	1
8	BRT	0	0	0	0	0	0	1	0	1	1	1	0	0	0	1	1	1	1	0	1	0	0	1	0
9	CHAM	0	0	1	0	0	1	1	1	0	1	1	0	1	1	0	1	0	1	1	1	1	1	1	0
10	GM	0	0	0	0	0	0	0	1	1	0	1	0	0	0	0	0	0	0	0	0	1	1	1	0
11	NAM	0	0	0	0	1	1	0	1	1	1	0	0	0	0	0	1	0	0	0	1	1	0	1	0
12	NEA	1	0	0	0	0	0	0	0	0	0	0	0	1	0	0	0	0	0	0	0	0	0	0	0
13	AARP	1	0	1	0	0	0	0	0	1	0	0	0	0	0	0	0	0	0	0	0	0	1	1	1
14	ACLU	1	0	0	0	0	0	0	0	1	0	0	1	1	0	0	0	0	0	0	0	0	0	0	1
15	NGA	1	0	0	0	0	0	0	0	0	0	0	1	0	0	0	1	1	1	0	1	0	0	0	0
16	DOLS	0	0	0	0	0	0	0	1	1	0	0	0	0	0	0	0	0	0	0	0	1	1	1	0
17	ETA	1	0	0	0	0	0	0	0	1	0	1	0	0	0	0	0	0	0	0	0	0	0	1	0
18	OSHA	0	0	1	1	0	1	1	0	0	0	0	0	0	0	0	1	0	0	0	0	0	0	0	0
19	NLRB	0	0	1	0	0	0	0	0	1	0	0	0	0	0	0	0	0	0	0	0	1	0	1	0
20	WHO	1	0	1	0	0	1	1	1	1	1	0	0	0	0	0	1	0	0	1	0	0	1	1	0
21	HR	0	0	1	0	0	0	0	1	1	1	1	0	0	0	0	1	0	0	1	0	0	1	0	0
22	HD	0	0	0	0	0	0	0	0	0	0	0	0	0	0	0	0	0	0	0	0	0	0	0	0
23	SR	0	0	0	0	0	0	0	0	0	0	0	0	0	0	0	0	0	0	0	0	0	0	0	0
24	SD	1	0	1	1	1	0	0	0	0	0	0	0	1	0	0	0	0	0	1	0	0	0	0	0

AFL: American Federation of Labor

ASCM: American Federation of State, County, and Municipal Workers

TEAM: Teamsters Union

UAW: United Auto Workers

USW: United Steel Workers

ABC: Association of Builders and Contractors

AGC: Association of General Contractors

BRT: Business Roundtable

CHAM: Chamber of Commerce of the United States

GM: General Motors

NAM: National Association of Manufacturers

NEA: National Education Association

AARP: American Association of Retired Persons

ACLU: American Civil Liberties Union

NGA: National Governors Association

DOLS: Department of Labor Secretary

ETA: DoL Education & Training Administration

OSHA: Occupational Safety & Health Administration

NLRB: National Labor Relations Board

WHO: White House Office

HR: House Labor Committee Republicans

HD: House Labor Committee Democrats

SR: Senate Labor Committee Republicans

SD: Senate Labor Committee Democrats

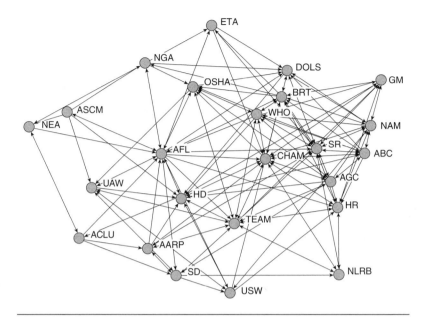

Figure 4.15   Digraph of U.S. National Labor Policy Domain

The composition of the jointly occupied blocks and their locations in the social map reflect a basic political cleavage between labor and capital in the late 20th-century United States. At the lower right of Figure 4.16, Block 1 is a pro-labor position consisting of four labor unions, including the peak AFL-CIO, an interest group representing the elderly (AARP), and Democrats on the Senate Labor Committee. The smaller Block 2 contains three interest groups and the ETA, an agency of the federal Labor Department. Block 3 is a pro-business position, occupied by the Reagan White House, the Department of Labor, three business associations, but also the Teamsters Union (not an AFL-CIO member). Block 4 is also largely a pro-business position, including the other three Congressional committees (two Republican groups but also the House Democrats) and two major peak business associations, the Business Roundtable and Chamber of Commerce of the U.S. According to the image matrix in Table 4.5, each block maintains high densities of internal policy communication, but only 3 of the 12 interblock densities indicate frequent ties: The pro-labor Block 1 sends policy information to the congressional

TABLE 4.5

Blocked, Density, and Image Matrices of Core Communication
Network in U.S. Labor Policy Domain

```
Blocked Matrix
                  2     1   1 1 1 1   1     2     1 1 1           2 2 2 1
                1 2 4 4 5 3   5 4 2 7   0 3 7 0 6 6 1 9     9 8 1 2 3 8
            --------------------------------------------------------------
  1  AFL  |  1 1 1 1   |  1        1 |  1           1 |  1 1 1 1 1 1 |
  2 ASCM  |  1   1     |  1 1        |             1  |         1    |
 24   SD  |  1   1 1 1 |             |     1        1 |           1  |
  4  UAW  |  1 1   1   |             |     1          |         1    |
  5  USW  |  1 1       |             |                |     1 1 1    |
 13 AARP  |  1 1       |             |     1          |  1        1 1|
            --------------------------------------------------------------
 15  NGA  |  1         |        1 1  |     1 1        |             1|
 14 ACLU  |  1 1   1   |        1    |                |  1           |
 12  NEA  |  1         |     1       |                |              |
 17  ETA  |  1         |             |           1    |  1        1  |
            --------------------------------------------------------------
 10   GM  |            |             |            1   |  1 1 1 1 1   |
  3 TEAM  |      1   1 |             |     1 1      1 |  1     1 1 1 1|
  7  AGC  |      1     |             |  1     1 1 1 1 |  1 1 1 1 1 1 |
 20  WHO  |  1         |             |1 1 1     1     |  1 1     1 1 1|
  6  ABC  |            |             |     1 1     1 1|  1 1 1 1 1 1 |
 16 DOLS  |            |             |                |  1 1 1 1 1   |
 11  NAM  |        1   |             |  1     1 1 1   |  1 1 1     1 |
 19 NLRB  |            |             |  1             |  1     1   1 |
            --------------------------------------------------------------
  9 CHAM  |        1   |  1          |1 1 1 1 1 1 1 1 |  1 1 1 1 1   |
  8  BRT  |            |  1        1 |1     1 1     1 1|  1        1 1|
 21   HR  |            |             |1 1         1 1 1|  1 1      1  |
 22   HD  |            |             |                |              |
 23   SR  |            |             |                |              |
 18 OSHA  |        1   |             |  1 1      1 1   |              |
            --------------------------------------------------------------
```

Density Matrix					Image Matrix			
	1	2	3	4		1	2	3	4
Block 1	0.567	0.167	0.125	0.389	Block 1	1	0	0	1
Block 2	0.250	0.333	0.094	0.167	Block 2	0	1	0	0
Block 3	0.104	0.000	0.393	0.813	Block 3	0	0	1	1
Block 4	0.056	0.125	0.458	0.367	Block 4	0	0	1	1

Block 4, and the congressional Block 4 and pro-business Block 3 mutually exchange information. Although the blockmodel and MDS analyses reveal a clear ideological divide, the presence of some organizations in unexpected positions (e.g., House Democrats and Teamsters) implies that policy contacts occur between opponents as well as among friends, perhaps moderating the intensity of political conflicts in the U.S. national labor policy domain.

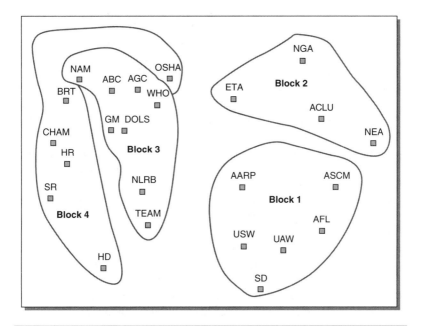

Figure 4.16   MDS With Blocks in U.S. National Labor Policy Domain (Stress = 0.20)

CHAPTER 5
ADVANCED METHODS FOR ANALYZING NETWORKS

This chapter discusses more advanced methods for analyzing social networks. In particular, we review network position measures, logit p*, affiliation networks, and the analysis of lattices.

5.1. Network Position Measures

Roles and positions are central concepts in social network analysis. Analyses of interlocking roles using algebraic and matrix methods began with S. F. Nadel's (1957) theory of social structure as positions possessing distinctive rights and duties in relation to other positions. Structural equivalence, discussed in Chapter 4, offers one basic approach to identifying roles and positions in a social network. However, its requirement that structurally equivalent actors must have identical patterns of ties to the same other actors is too stringent for much practical use. Although loosening the criterion to permit relational similarities broadens its applicability, structural equivalence still imposes a very restrictive notion of which actors jointly occupy positions based on their relational patterns. As an alternative, network researchers developed several less-restrictive approaches to identifying roles and positions (Borgatti & Everett, 1992; Everett, 1985; Everett, Boyd, & Borgatti, 1990; Faust, 1988; Pattison, 1988). In decreasing order of restrictiveness, structural equivalence is the most restrictive, followed by automorphic and isomorphic equivalence, then regular equivalence. This section provides a nontechnical overview of those latter methods. For simplicity of illustration, we examine a nondirected binary graph of a single relation, although, with some modifications, both automorphic and isomorphic equivalence can be applied to directed and valued graphs (Wasserman & Faust, 1994, pp. 461–502).

Isomorphic and automorphic equivalence are such closely related concepts that some researchers treat them as interchangeable (Borgatti & Everett, 1992). However, isomorphic equivalence applies to two graphs, whereas automorphic equivalence describes the relational properties of social actors within one graph. Two graphs exhibit structural *isomorphism* if a one-to-one mapping of the nodes from one graph onto the second graph preserves all the nodes' adjacency relations (i.e., the same indegrees and outdegrees). In other words, if two nodes are connected in the first graph, then the corresponding two nodes in the second graph must also be connected in the same way (Borgatti & Everett, 1992, p. 11). Every graph is isomorphic with itself, which is called *automorphism*, a one-to-one mapping of nodes back onto themselves. Two actors are *automorphically equivalent* (jointly occupy the same position) if and only if they are connected to corresponding other positions (but *not* to identical nodes). Automorphic equivalent nodes have identical graph theoretic properties, such as centrality, ego-density, and clique size (Borgatti & Everett, 1992).

Automorphic equivalence relaxes the structural equivalence requirement that actors in the same position have identical or very similar ties with the same set of other actors. Instead, automorphic equivalence identifies actors as jointly occupying a position if they have identical ties with different sets of actors that play the same role in relation to that position. To use a familiar example, for two professors to occupy a structurally equivalent position, both must teach the identical set of students, which is a virtual impossibility. But, to occupy an automorphically equivalent position, the two professors need only teach different sets with the same number of students. The students occupy a second position, defined as persons taught by the professor position. The graphs in Figure 5.1 contrast these two types of equivalence, where directed lines from professors to students represent the "teach" relation. Although both graphs have two positions, automorphic equivalence better captures the idea that social roles involve generalized patterns of relations. To cite another well-known instance, in monogamous marriages, we expect the wife position to be jointly occupied by a set of women who are in nonplural marriages to the same set of men, but who are each uniquely paired with a different husband!

Structurally equivalent actors are also automorphically equivalent, but not necessarily vice versa. Automorphically equivalent nodes are indistinguishable if the actor labels are removed from a graph. Thus, if points are substituted for the names in Figure 5.1B, the two subgraphs cannot be told apart. Borgatti and Everett (1992, p. 16) summarized the distinction:

> Abstracting a bit, we could say that in the structural equivalence approach, the network or labeled graph represents the underlying structure of a group; hence an actor's location in that structure represents his or her position in the group. In contrast, in the [automorphic equivalence] approach, the structure of interest is not the labeled graph itself, which is seen as the observed or "surface structure," but the structure of the surface structure, which is the unlabeled graph that underlies the labeled graph. It is the actor's location in this "deep structure," then, that represents his or her position in the group.

By relaxing the structural equivalence requirements, automorphic equivalence becomes very useful in facilitating empirical research corresponding to many social theories. Borgatti and Everett (1992) argued that several studies which operationalized theories using structural equivalence would be better analyzed using automorphic equivalence. For example, they addressed Burt's (1979) proposal to define the industries and sectors of an economy as sets of firms that produce similar types of goods and occupy a single position within an interorganizational network. Borgatti and Everett (1992, p. 21) asserted that structurally equivalent firms, which by definition must buy from the same providers and sell to the same clients, hardly constitute recognizable sectors. But automorphically equivalent firms, which buy from similar vendors and sell to similar customers, might well comprise meaningful industries and sectors.

Regular equivalence is the least restrictive of the three most commonly used forms of equivalence. It requires neither structural equivalence's ties to identical actors nor automorphic equivalence's indistinguishable positions. Actors are regularly equivalent if they have the same kinds of relations with actors that are also regularly equivalent. Another way to conceptualize the idea is that, if a first actor occupying a position is tied to someone in a second position, then a regularly equivalent second actor must have an identical tie to someone else in a second position (White & Reitz,

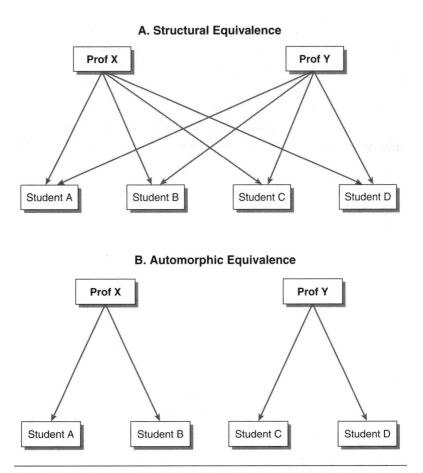

Figure 5.1   Structural Equivalence Versus Automorphic Equivalence

1983, p. 214). All mothers with children are regularly equivalent, regardless of their numbers of offspring, as are all children who have mothers. In a hospital, the doctors are regularly equivalent in relation to their patients and nurses, even when the numbers of patients and nurses per doctor differ. The generality of regular equivalence makes it perhaps the most important measure for sociologists attempting to capture social roles and positions.

Both automorphic equivalence and regular equivalence require that a pair of actors connect with the other actors who are structurally equivalent on the same relation. However, the distinction between automorphic and regular equivalence is sometimes ambiguous. Automorphic equivalence

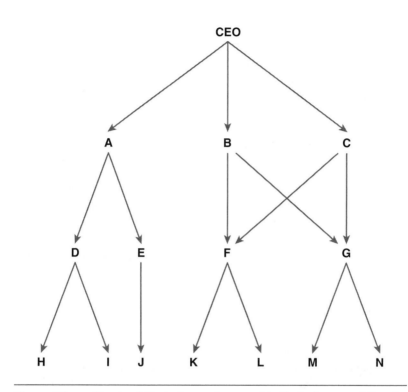

Figure 5.2 Structural Equivalence, Automorphic Equivalence, and Regular
Equivalence in an Organizational Hierarchy

requires that unlabeled graphs be strictly substitutable for one another, but
regular equivalence does not require a complete substitutability between
subgraphs.

To demonstrate the difference, Figure 5.2 depicts a hierarchical organizational chart consisting of four vertical levels linked by supervisory
relations. The CEO supervises three executive managers (A, B, C), who
supervise four middle managers (D, E, F, G), who in turn supervise a few
front-line employees (H through N). If we ignore the employees, then
executive managers B and C are structurally equivalent because both have
identical supervisory ties to the same middle managers (F and G). But A is
not structurally equivalent to B and C, because A supervises different middle managers. However, the three executives are regularly equivalent,
because each supervises the same number of middle managers (two apiece).
If we consider all hierarchical levels, B and C are also automorphically

equivalent because their subgraphs are substitutable for one another if the labels were removed. But A's subgraph cannot be substituted for B's or C's subgraphs, since A's two middle managers supervise only three front-line employees, whereas both B's and C's subgraphs each have four employees.

Considering only the two lowest levels, none of the four middle managers are structurally equivalent, because they all supervise different front-line employees. Instead, three of the middle managers (D, F, and G) are automorphically equivalent, because their two-employee subgraphs are completely substitutable once the labels are removed (unlike E, who supervises only one employee). But all four middle managers meet the regular equivalence criterion by supervising at least one employee. Figure 5.2 demonstrates that structural equivalence is the most restrictive form, regular equivalence is the least strict, and automorphic equivalence lies in between. Regular equivalence seems a very flexible method for identifying generalized social roles in networks, broadly defined as aggregate classes or categories of actors having similar structural relations with other positions in a social system (Faust, 1988, p. 315).

5.2. Logit Models (p^*)

Most social network methods are descriptive, attempting to represent some underlying social structures through data reduction techniques or to characterize network properties through algebraic computations. An important statistical method, p^* models, moves beyond description to explain the presence of dyadic ties as a function of individual- and graph-level explanatory factors. Wasserman and Pattison (1996) initially proposed the p^* model, emerging from earlier treatises on Markov random graphs (Frank & Strauss, 1986), log-linear models of directed graphs (p1) (Holland & Leinhardt, 1981), and algorithms for implementing pseudo-likelihood estimation (Strauss & Ikeda, 1990). In subsequent developments, the p^* family of models was extended to analyze multivariate relations (Pattison & Wasserman, 1999) and valued relations (Robins, Pattison, & Wasserman, 1999). Two applications of p^* described the data structure and interpretation of the results (Anderson, Wasserman, & Crouch 1999; Crouch & Wasserman, 1998), with a third providing an accessible introduction (Wasserman & Robins, 2005). This section briefly discusses the basic p^* model, illustrating with an application to an artificial network (Crouch & Wasserman, 1998, pp. 87–101). Although the approach can analyze multivariate relations and valued graphs, for simplicity we presume a binary digraph of a single relation. Interested readers should consult the preceding references for more advanced treatments.

The p* model is closely related to logistic regression. Logistic regression analyzes a dichotomous dependent variable [coded as a binary variable: $Y = 1$ or $Y = 0$] that is presumed to have a binomial distribution. If ordinary least squares regression methods were applied to model the probability of Y as a function of the linear combination of independent variables, two major problems would arise: (1) some predicted probabilities might be higher than 1.0 or lower than 0.0, obviously nonsensical values; and (2) key assumptions about the error term would be violated, specifically that it is normally distributed with constant variance (homoscedasticity), and is uncorrelated with the independent variables. The logistic regression model avoids these problems by transforming probabilities into logits, specifically:

$$\text{logit } (Y) = \ln\left(\frac{\Pr(Y=1)}{\Pr(Y=0)}\right) = \beta_0 + \beta_1 X_1 + \beta_2 X_2 + \cdots + \beta_k X_k \quad (5.1)$$

With appropriate transformations, the β parameters can be interpreted as effects of the independent variables on the logit, odds, or probability of Y. The odds transformation is most common, possibly because it is more straightforward than the logit and less complex than the probability method (Pampel, 2000). To obtain the effects of independent variables on the odds, exponentiate both sides of the preceding equation:

$$\frac{\Pr(Y=1)}{\Pr(Y=0)} = \exp(\beta_0 + \beta_1 X_1 + \beta_2 X_2 + \cdots + \beta_k X_k)$$
$$= e^{\beta_0} e^{\beta_1 y_1} \ldots e^{\beta_k y_k} \quad (5.2)$$

This equation shows that the independent variables exert multiplicative impacts on the odds of a case being in category 1 relative to category 0 of the dependent variable. Interpreting the net effect of the ith independent variable on the odds involves exponentiating the original parameter e^{β_k}.

The p* model applies logistic regression to social network data. For a single-relation network with dichotomous directed ties among g actors, the (i,j) cell entry in $g \times g$ matrix $\mathbf{X}$ is a binary value:

$$x_{i,j} = \begin{cases} 1 & \text{if } i \to j \\ 0 & \text{otherwise} \end{cases}$$

Wasserman and Pattison (1996) proposed three additional matrices: (1) $\mathbf{X}_{i,j}^+$ for the relational tie from i to j, which is forced to be present; (2) $\mathbf{X}_{i,j}^-$ for the relational tie from i to j, which is forced to be absent; and (3) $\mathbf{X}_{i,j}^C$ for the complementary tie from i to j. Using these matrices, the probability that the tie from i to j is present, conditional on the complementary tie, is the following:

$$Pr(x_{i,j} = 1|x_{ij}^C) = \frac{Pr(x = x_{ij}^+)}{Pr(x = x_{ij}^+) + Pr(x = x_{ij}^-)}$$

$$= \frac{\exp\{\theta Z(x_{ij}^+)\}}{\exp\{\theta Z(x_{ij}^+)\} + \exp\{\theta Z(x_{ij}^-)\}} \quad (5.3)$$

In the second expression, θ is a vector of effect parameters to be estimated, whereas $Z(x_{ij}^+)$ and $Z(x_{ij}^-)$ are vectors of raw data for various independent or explanatory variables.

The odds ratio of a present tie to an absent tie from i to j is the following:

$$\frac{Pr(x_{i,j} = 1|x_{ij}^C)}{Pr(x_{i,j} = 0|x_{ij}^C)} = \frac{\exp\{\theta Z(x_{ij}^+)\}}{\exp\{\theta Z(x_{ij}^-)\}} \quad (5.4)$$

Taking the natural log of both sides and simplifying transforms the equation to the following:

$$\log\left[\frac{Pr(x_{i,j} = 1|x_{ij}^C)}{Pr(x_{i,j} = 0|x_{ij}^C)}\right] = \theta \left[Z(x_{ij}^+) - Z(x_{ij}^-)\right] \quad (5.5)$$

This equation, called p*, contains a vector of effect parameters θ to be estimated, and a vector of raw data when the variable $x_{i,j}$ is forced to change from 1 to 0.

Several issues in the p* model require explication. First, the units of analysis are dyads in a complete network; thus, for a directed graph with N actors, the total number of cases is $N^2 - N$. Second, although the model appears to estimate dyadic properties, it is a model of the entire graph. In particular, the p* model assesses the conditional probability of observing the current graph as a function of various network properties, treated as independent variables, such as choice, mutuality, and transitivity. Third, the values of those independent variables are the differences of the aggregated values of those variables for the entire graph when a given tie from i to j is forced to be changed from being present to being absent. For example, suppose the total number of mutual ties in a particular graph is five. If the tie of a specific pair is present, say from Actor 4 to 5, then forcing the tie from 4 to 5 to be absent would eliminate one mutual tie of this graph. Thus, the value of the independent variable "mutuality" for the pair (4 ↔ 5) should be 1. The p* model essentially estimates the probability of observing the current graph if ties (x_{ij}) were to form at random, and if each directed tie had an independent probability of occurring.

To illustrate a p* model, we use the same binary digraph as Crouch and Wasserman (1998). Figure 5.3 shows "programming support to" relations

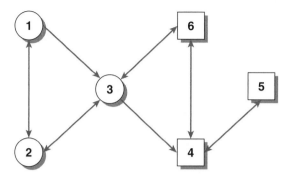

Figure 5.3   Digraph of Programming Support Among Three Governmental
Research Organizations (Circles) and Three Private R&D Labs
(Squares)

among three governmental research organizations (circles) and three private R&D labs (squares). For example, governmental research organizations 1 and 2 reciprocate programming support to one another. Although research organization 3 provides programming support to private R&D lab 4, the tie is not reciprocated—lab 4 does not provide programming support to organization 3.

Programming support appears to occur more often within types, that is, among governmental research organizations and among private labs, than between types. To model this "same-type" hypothesis, as well as hypotheses about other network relations about the presence of ties, Crouch and Wasserman (1998) modeled five p* parameters: (1) overall degree of choice (θ); (2) differential choice within type (θ_w); (3) mutuality (ρ); (4) differential mutuality within type (ρ_w); and (5) transitivity (τ_T), where a relation is transitive if every time that i directs a relation to j and j directs a relation to k, then i also directs a relation to $k (i \rightarrow j, j \rightarrow k, i \rightarrow k)$ (Wasserman & Faust, 1994, p. 165). In our substantive example, we are interested in whether programming support occurs more often among same-type organizations, and whether support is more often reciprocated among same-type organizations than between organizations of different types. Thus, the vector of parameters to be estimated is the following:

$$\theta = \{\theta, \theta_w, \rho, \rho_w, \tau_T\}$$

Estimating the vector of explanatory variables for all pairs of actors in the digraph involves calculating the changes in the vector of raw data $Z(x)$, when the ties between i and j are forced to change from 1 to 0. In particular,

$Z_\theta = \sum X_{ij}$ is the choice explanatory variable,

$Z_{\theta_w} = \sum X_{ij}\delta_{ij}$ is the choice within-type variable,

$Z_\rho = \sum_{i<j} x_{ij}x_{ji}$ is the mutuality variable,

$Z_{\rho_w} = \sum_{i<j} x_{ij}x_{ji}\delta_{ij}$ is the mutuality within-type variable, and

$Z_{\tau_T} = \sum_{ijk} X_{ij}X_{jk}X_{ik}$ is the transitivity variable.

The indicator variable δ_{ij} is a binary indicator that equals 1 if i and j are the same type and 0 if otherwise. For a digraph of g nodes, the total number of ordered pairs for the p* model are $g(g-1) = g^2 - g$. Thus, the six organizations comprise 30 ordered pairs. Space limitation prohibits an exposition of the full p* model parameters. Interested readers should consult Anderson et al. (1999) and Wasserman and Pattison (1996).

Table 5.1 contains the input dataset for estimating p* parameters for the 30 ordered pairs. The following example illustrates how to compute values of the input dataset by applying the five formulas to one ordered dyad, $(2 \rightarrow 3)$, the directed tie from Actor 2 to Actor 3 in the seventh row in the table. First, the choice variable is computed by subtracting the total number of ties when a tie from actor i to j is forced to be absent from the total number of ties when a tie from actor i and j is forced to be present $(\sum X_{ij}^+ - \sum X_{ij}^-)$. The choice variable in the example is 1 for every dyad. Thus, the choice variable is actually a constant, equivalent to the model intercept. Second, the choice within the same type for Actor 2 to Actor 3 is 1, because the total number of choices within the same type is 9 if the tie from Actor 2 to Actor 3 is forced to be present, and the total is 8 if that tie is forced to be absent. The mutual tie between Actor 3 and 6 and the direct tie from Actor 3 to Actor 4 do not count because both dyads are cross-types. Third, the digraph has five mutual ties $(1\leftrightarrow2, 2\leftrightarrow3, 3\leftrightarrow6, 4\leftrightarrow6, 4\leftrightarrow5)$. Forcing the direct tie from Actor 2 to Actor 3 to be absent reduces the total number of mutual ties to 4. Thus, the value of the mutuality variable from Actor 2 to Actor 3 is $5 - 4 = 1$. Fourth, the digraph has four mutual ties within the same type $(1\leftrightarrow2, 2\leftrightarrow3, 4\leftrightarrow6, 4\leftrightarrow5)$, excluding the mutual tie between Actor 3 and Actor 6, which is cross-type. Thus, forcing the directed tie from Actor 2 to Actor 3 to be absent reduces the total mutuality within the same type by $4 - 3 = 1$. Fifth, the digraph has five transitive relations $[(1 \rightarrow 2, 2 \rightarrow 3, 1 \rightarrow 3), (1 \rightarrow 3, 3 \rightarrow 2, 1 \rightarrow 2), (2 \rightarrow 1, 1 \rightarrow 3, 2 \rightarrow 3), (3 \rightarrow 6, 6 \rightarrow 4, 3 \rightarrow 4), \text{ and } (3 \rightarrow 4, 4 \rightarrow 6, 3 \rightarrow 6)]$. Forcing the directed tie from Actor 2 to Actor 3 to be absent eliminates two transitive relations, $(1 \rightarrow 2, 2 \rightarrow 3, 1 \rightarrow 3)$ and $(2 \rightarrow 1, 1 \rightarrow 3, 2 \rightarrow 3)$. Hence, the

TABLE 5.1
p* Dataset

Obs.	i	j	Tie	Choice	Choice-Within	Mutuality	Mutuality-Within	Transitivity
1	1	2	1	1	1	1	1	2
2	1	3	1	1	1	0	0	3
3	1	4	0	1	0	0	0	1
4	1	5	0	1	0	0	0	0
5	1	6	0	1	0	0	0	2
6	2	1	1	1	1	1	1	1
7	2	3	1	1	1	1	1	2
8	2	4	0	1	0	0	0	2
9	2	5	0	1	0	0	0	0
10	2	6	0	1	0	0	0	3
11	3	1	0	1	1	1	1	3
12	3	2	1	1	1	1	1	1
13	3	4	1	1	0	0	0	3
14	3	5	0	1	0	0	0	2
15	3	6	1	1	0	1	0	2
16	4	1	0	1	0	0	0	0
17	4	2	0	1	0	0	0	1
18	4	3	0	1	0	1	0	3
19	4	5	1	1	1	1	1	0
20	4	6	1	1	1	1	1	1
21	5	1	0	1	0	0	0	0
22	5	2	0	1	0	0	0	0
23	5	3	0	1	0	0	0	1
24	5	4	1	1	1	1	1	0
25	5	6	0	1	1	0	0	3
26	6	1	0	1	0	0	0	1
27	6	2	0	1	0	0	0	3
28	6	3	1	1	0	1	0	1
29	6	4	1	1	1	1	1	2
30	6	5	0	1	1	0	0	3

value for the transitivity variable is 2. In summary, the five computations for the ordered dyad $(2 \to 3)$ are the following:

Change in choice $\sum X_{ij}^{+} - \sum X_{ij}^{-} = 1$.

Change in choice within the same type

$$\sum X_{ij}^{+} \delta_{ij} - \sum X_{ij}^{-} \delta_{ij} = 9 - 8 = 1.$$

Change in mutuality $\sum_{i<j}^{+} x_{ij} x_{ji} - \sum_{i<j}^{-} x_{ij} x_{ji} = 5 - 4 = 1.$

TABLE 5.2
Unstandardized Logistic Regression of Network Ties

Variables	Model 1
Choice	−2.208
	(1.197)
Choice-within same type	2.741
	(2.183)
Mutuality	3.737*
	(1.829)
Mutuality within same type	−1.588
	(2.921)
Transitivity	−0.408
	(1.197)
chi-square (*df*)	19.488***(4)
−2 log likelihood	20.893

Note. Numbers in parentheses are standard errors.
* $p < .05$, ** $p < .01$, *** $p < .001$ (two-tailed test)

Change in mutuality within the same type

$$\sum\nolimits_{i<j}^{+} x_{ij}x_{ji}\delta_{ij} - \sum\nolimits_{i<j}^{-} x_{ij}x_{ji}\delta_{ij} = 4 - 3 = 1.$$

Change in the transitivity

$$\sum\nolimits_{ijk}^{+} X_{ij}X_{jk}X_{ik} - \sum\nolimits_{ijk}^{-} X_{ij}X_{jk}X_{ik} = 5 - 3 = 2.$$

The data in Table 5.1 can be analyzed using the logistic regression program of a statistical software package, such as SPSS, SAS, or STATA. The dependent variable is the binary variable "tie," which is regressed on the five independent variables—choice, choice-within type, mutuality, mutuality-within type, and transitivity. Table 5.2 shows the results. Only one explanatory variable—mutuality ties—is significant. Each unit increase in the mutuality ties involving a directed tie from i to j increases the odds that i sends a tie to j by almost 41 times ($\exp(3.737) - 1 = 40.97$). The odds that a mutual tie is present are 41 times greater than its absence, holding constant the other explanatory variables (Anderson et al., 1999, p. 54). Thus, ties in this digraph are far more likely to be reciprocated than not. However, reciprocity and choice do not differ by type of organization; neither "choice within the same type" nor "mutuality within the same type" is significant. The results do not support the hypothesis that provision of programming support occurs more often among same-type organizations than between different types of organizations.

The development of p* models marked an important advance in social network analysis methods. It moves beyond representation and description, toward the explanation of relational ties between actors. It explicitly models the impacts on relational ties of graph-level characteristics and individual variables. Immense opportunities lie ahead for network researchers to use p* and similar methods to analyze substantive social issues. Some didactic texts with many substantive illustrations of p* would be helpful in propagating this approach to network researchers.

5.3. Affiliation Networks

Affiliation networks, also called membership networks, represent the involvement of a set of actors in a set of social events (Wasserman & Faust, 1994, pp. 291–343). Persons may be linked through their joint participation in social activities or by their common membership in organizations. Conversely, social events are connected to the extent that they have actors in common. Affiliation network analysis visualizes how actors and events are simultaneously interrelated.

An affiliation network consists of two types of nodes—a set of actors and a set of events—and a set of relations between each nodal type. Thus, an affiliation network is a *two-mode network*, in contrast to a *one-mode network* linking actors to actors. Substantive studies of affiliation networks are numerous (Wasserman & Faust, 1994, p. 196). In Chapter 3 we discussed the Freeman et al. (1987) research on university faculty and students who attended nine colloquia. The researchers used affiliation networks to represent these relations, in which people are actors and colloquia are events. Other familiar examples are members belonging to voluntary associations, social movement activists participating in protests, firms creating strategic alliances, and nations signing military treaties. Research on two-mode affiliation networks often has dual objectives: to uncover the relational structures among actors through their joint involvement in events, and to reveal the relational structures of events attracting common participants.

Affiliation Matrix and Bipartite Graph. A binary affiliation network can be formally represented by an *affiliation matrix* that records the presence and absence of g actors at h events; thus, its dimensions are g rows and h columns, respectively. If actor i attends event j, the entry in the i, jth cell in the matrix equals 1; otherwise the entry is 0. Denoting a binary affiliation matrix as **A,** its x_{ij} values meet these conditions:

$$x_{i,j} = \begin{cases} 1 & \text{if actor } i \text{ is affiliated with event } j \\ 0 & \text{otherwise} \end{cases}$$

104

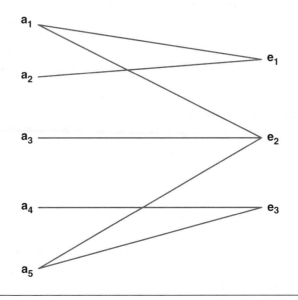

Figure 5.4   Bipartite Graph of an Affiliation Network

The row totals, also called row marginals, of matrix **A** sum to the number of events that each actor attended ($\sum_{j=1}^{h} x_{i,j}$). The column marginals ($\sum_{i=1}^{g} x_{i,j}$) indicate the number of actors who attended each event.

An affiliation network may also be displayed as a *bipartite graph*, in which nondirected lines connect actors aligned on one side of the diagram to the events aligned on the other side. Importantly, a bipartite graph does not permit lines among the actors nor among the events. A *bipartite matrix* (**B**) contains both sets of actors and events in the rows and columns. Assuming an affiliation network has *g* actors and *h* events, **B** has dimensions $(g+h) \times (g+h)$.

Figure 5.4 is a bipartite graph of an affiliation network with five actors and three events. The lines indicate which actors attended which events, as well as which events drew which actors. Although the graph contains no lines directly connecting actors with events, it suggests how actors are linked via their common affiliations with specific events. For example, Actor 1 and Actor 2 both participated in Event 1, and Actors 1, 3, and 5 were all involved in Event 2.

Table 5.3 is the bipartite matrix corresponding to the graph in Figure 5.4, where a cell value of 1 indicates that an actor and an event are affiliated.

TABLE 5.3
Bipartite Matrix of the Graph in Figure 5.4

	a1	*a2*	*a3*	*a4*	*a5*	*e1*	*e2*	*e3*	*Row Total*
a1	—	0	0	0	0	**1**	**1**	**0**	2
a2	0	—	0	0	0	**1**	**0**	**0**	1
a3	0	0	—	0	0	**0**	**1**	**0**	1
a4	0	0	0	—	0	**0**	**0**	**1**	1
a5	0	0	0	0	—	**0**	**1**	**1**	2
e1	**1**	**1**	**0**	**0**	**0**	—	0	0	2
e2	**1**	**0**	**1**	**0**	**1**	0	—	0	3
e3	**0**	**0**	**0**	**1**	**1**	0	0	—	2
Column Total	2	1	1	1	2	2	3	2	—

Actor 1 has two 1s, showing that it attended both Event 1 and Event 2. The 5×3 submatrix in the upper right quadrant, consisting of the five actors in the rows and the three events in the columns, is the affiliation matrix **A**. The lower left quadrant is the transpose of **A**, denoted as $\mathbf{A}'$ (with dimensions 3×5 and $x_{i,j} = x_{j,i}$). A transposed affiliation matrix shows which events in the rows attracted which participants in the columns. The other two quadrants of a bipartite matrix always have only 0s in their cells, because, in two-mode data, the actors are not directly linked to one another, nor are the events. A bipartite matrix can be schematically represented as the following:

$$\mathbf{X}^{A, E} = \begin{bmatrix} 0 & \mathbf{A} \\ \mathbf{A}' & 0 \end{bmatrix} \qquad (5.6)$$

At the margins of the table, but not properly part of the matrix, the row totals equal the column totals. The total for an actor shows how many events it attended, while an event total indicates the number of actors who participated.

Multiplying the two submatrices (**A** and $\mathbf{A}'$) in two different orders yields additional information, about relations among the actors and among the events, that is not available in a bipartite matrix. First, $\mathbf{X}^A$ is a symmetric, valued matrix of coattendance for pairs of actors, obtained as the product of matrix multiplication:

$$\mathbf{X}^A = \mathbf{A}\mathbf{A}' \qquad (5.7)$$

In general, affiliation network **A** is a $g \times h$ matrix, and its transpose $\mathbf{A}'$ is an $h \times g$ matrix. Thus, $\mathbf{X}^A$ is always a $g \times g$ matrix, whose nondiagonal cell values are the numbers of events attended by both actor i and actor j. The diagonal entries of **A** show the number of events each actor attended.

Second, $\mathbf{X}^{\mathbf{E}}$ is a symmetric, valued matrix of coparticipants for pairs of events, obtained by multiplying the matrices in reverse order:

$$\mathbf{X}^{\mathbf{E}} = \mathbf{A}'\mathbf{A} \tag{5.8}$$

The nondiagonal cell values of this $h \times h$ matrix are the number of actors participating in both event i and event j, while the diagonal entries of $\mathbf{A}'$ are the number of actors attending each event.

The coattendance matrix for the example data is the following:

$$\mathbf{X}^A = \mathbf{AA}' = \begin{pmatrix} 110 \\ 100 \\ 010 \\ 001 \\ 011 \end{pmatrix} \times \begin{pmatrix} 11000 \\ 10101 \\ 00011 \end{pmatrix} = \begin{pmatrix} 21101 \\ 11000 \\ 10101 \\ 00011 \\ 10112 \end{pmatrix} \tag{5.9}$$

With five actors and three events, the resulting $\mathbf{X}^A$ is a 5×5 symmetric matrix whose nondiagonal cell values show the number of events attended by each dyad. As shown by the first row, Actor 1 attended one event each with Actors 2, 3, and 5, but no events with Actor 4. The diagonal shows that Actors 1 and 5 each attended two events and the others attended one apiece.

The coparticipation matrix for the example is the following:

$$\mathbf{X}^{\mathbf{E}} = \mathbf{A}'\mathbf{A} = \begin{pmatrix} 11000 \\ 10101 \\ 00011 \end{pmatrix} \times \begin{pmatrix} 110 \\ 100 \\ 010 \\ 001 \\ 011 \end{pmatrix} = \begin{pmatrix} 210 \\ 131 \\ 012 \end{pmatrix} \tag{5.10}$$

The nondiagonal cells of this 3×3 symmetric matrix show the number of actors attending each pair of events. Events 1 and 2 had one actor in common (Actor 1 attended both events), but Events 1 and 3 shared no common actors. The diagonal values reveal that Event 2 attracted a total of three actors (Actors 1, 3, and 5).

At the network level of analysis, mean rates of affiliation are readily computed from values in the two product matrices. Because the diagonal entries of $\mathbf{X}^A$ are the numbers of events attendance by each actor, summing them and dividing by the number of actors (g) yields the mean actor atten-

dance rate, $\bar{\mathbf{X}}^A = \dfrac{\sum\limits_{i=1}^{g} x_{i,i}}{g}$. In the example, an average of $(\frac{7}{5}) = 1.40$ actors attended each event. Likewise, summing the diagonal values of $\mathbf{X}^{\mathbf{E}}$ and dividing by the total number of events (h) results in the mean event participation rate, $\bar{X}^E = \dfrac{\sum\limits_{i=1}^{h} X_{i,i}}{h}$. The mean participation at events in the example was $\left(\frac{7}{3}\right) = 2.33$ actors.

Density and Centrality in Affiliation Networks. Density and centrality are important basic network properties that also apply to affiliation networks. As discussed in Chapter 4, density measures reveal either the proportion of ties present in a binary graph, or the average value of the observed lines in a valued graph. Similarly, the interpretation of density for an affiliation network depends on whether an affiliation network is a binary or valued graph (Wasserman & Faust, 1994, pp. 316).

For a symmetric $g \times g$ coattendance matrix, $\mathbf{X}^A$, whose nondiagonal values are the number of events attended by each pair of actors, the density measure is the following:

$$D^A = \frac{\sum\limits_{i=1}^{g} \sum\limits_{j=1}^{g} \mathbf{X}_{ij}^A}{g(g-1)/2} \quad (i < j) \tag{5.11}$$

The numerator sums all the values in the upper triangle of the coattendance matrix (i.e., above the diagonal, because the lower triangle values are identical). The diagonal values are excluded because we cannot consider an actor as attending an event with itself. The denominator is the total number of nonordered dyads, again excluding the diagonal. For a symmetric $h \times h$ coparticipation matrix, $\mathbf{X}^E$, whose nondiagonal values are the number of actors participating in each event, the density measure is the following:

$$D^E = \frac{\sum\limits_{i=1}^{h} \sum\limits_{j}^{h} X_{i,j}^E}{h(h-1)/2} \quad (i < j) \tag{5.12}$$

In the example, $D^A = 5/10 = 0.50$, meaning that the pairs of actors jointly attended a mean of one half of an event. From event perspective, $D^E = 2/3 = 0.67$, indicating that the average pair of events attracted two thirds of an actor. Because a product matrix can have cell values greater than 1, densities could be larger than 1.0. Consequently, each density value should be interpreted not as a proportion, but as either the average number of events two actors attended (D^A) or the average number of actors present at two events (D^E), respectively.

Social network analysts have studied centrality at the actor level and centralization at the graph level of analysis for decades (Freeman, 1979; Wasserman & Faust, 1994, chap. 3). We commented in Chapter 4 that actor centrality measures the importance or visibility of actors within a network.

Depending on how they conceptualize importance or visibility, researchers describe four major types of centrality: degree, closeness, betweenness, and eigenvector centrality. Degree centrality reflects the extent to which an actor is active in a network; closeness centrality measures the extent to which an actor is connected with other actors in a network via shortest paths; betweenness centrality captures the extent to which an actor mediates flows of information or resources between other actors in a network; and eigenvector centrality reflects the extent to which an actor is connected to other central actors in a network. Faust (1997) discussed application of these four centrality measures to affiliation networks, but space constraints allow us to cover only degree centrality in affiliation networks.

Drawing on the general idea that degree centrality involves the total number of direct ties, actor degree centrality in an affiliation network is the total number of actor contacts that the ith actor has through its attendance at all events, obtained by summing the ith row of the coattendance matrix, $\mathbf{X^A}$:

$$C_D^A(a_i) = \sum_{j=1}^{g} x_{ij}^A \quad (i \neq j) \tag{5.13}$$

In the example, Actor 1 attended one event each with Actors 2, 3, and 5, so its degree centrality is 3. Actor 2 has lower degree centrality, because it only attended the first event with Actor 1.

Likewise, an event's degree centrality in an affiliation network is the total number of event contacts that the jth event has through the participation of all actors, obtained by summing the jth column of the coparticipation matrix, $\mathbf{X^E}$:

$$C_D^E(e_i) = \sum_{j=1}^{h} x_{ij}^E \quad (i \neq j) \tag{5.14}$$

The degree centralities for the three events are 1, 2, and 1, respectively. Event 2 has the highest degree centrality because it is connected to both Events 1 and 3 by the participation of at least one common actor, whereas Events 1 and 3 each share actors only with event 2.

5.4. Lattices

One clear advantage of affiliation networks, discussed in the preceding section, lies in visualizing three types of network structures in two-mode data: actor-by-event relations and the transpose, relations among actors via their joint attendance at events, and relations among events by their attraction of common participants. However, bipartite graphs of an affiliation network fail to reveal how both the actor and event nodes are related to one another. Galois lattices provide a general representation of two-mode data, creating a simultaneous visualization of the relations between both modes, which may yield valuable insights into the structural properties of a network (Freeman & White, 1993; Wasserman & Faust, 1994, pp. 326–342). Substantive applications include the relations between villagers and political disputes in revolutionary China (Schweizer, 1996), clients and treatments provided by agencies for poor relief (Mohr & Duquenne, 1997), and organizations and events in the 1992 Brazilian impeachment movement (Mische & Pattison, 2000).

Galois Lattices. Originating in the work of the 19th-century French mathematician Évariste Galois, the eponymous *Galois lattice*, also called Galois connection, is a correspondence between two partially ordered sets. In network applications, a Galois lattice has two nonempty sets: actor set A and event set E. The two sets are linked by the two-mode affiliation network indicating how the actors are related to the events (and vice versa). Therefore, a Galois lattice is defined with a triple (A, E, I), in which I is the binary relation in the matrix A × E. The submatrix A in the bipartite matrix in Table 5.3 is an example actor-by-event matrix. Now considering $P(A) = \{A_1, A_2, \ldots\}$, a collection of subsets of A, and $P(E) = \{E_1, E_2, \ldots\}$, a collection of subsets of E, the I relation defines the mapping from $P(A)$ to $P(E):B \rightarrow B \uparrow$:

$$B \uparrow = \{e \in E | (a, e) \in I \text{ for all } a \in A\} \tag{5.15}$$

This mathematical expression states that the mapping can identify all the events with which a specific actor or actors are affiliated. In particular, the $\uparrow$ mapping goes from a subset of actors to that subset of events with which all the actors in the subset are affiliated (Wasserman & Faust, 1994, p. 330). For example, the submatrix A in Table 5.3 shows that Actor 1 is affiliated with both Events 1 and 2, whereas both Actors 1 and 2 are affiliated with Event 1.

Conversely, the mapping can take place from $P(E)$ to $P(A): F \rightarrow F \downarrow$

$$F \downarrow = \{a \in A | (a, e) \in I \text{ for all } e \in E\} \tag{5.16}$$

This expression means the mapping should identify all the actors attracted to a specific event or events. The submatrix A in Table 5.3 shows that Event 2 attracts Actors 1, 3, and 5, whereas Events 2 and 3 attract only Actor 5.

Combining both mappings, the Galois lattice displays how subsets of actors are affiliated with subsets of events. Each point on the diagram represents both a subset of actors and a subset of events. To interpret a Galois

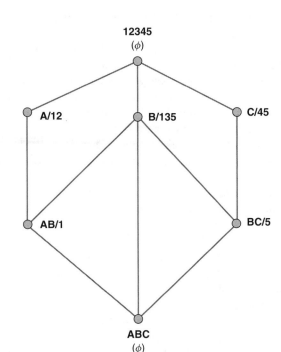

Figure 5.5   Galois Lattice of an Affiliation Network

lattice, always move in a consistent direction: (1) To trace the actors attending events, move only in an upward direction, ascending the lattice from bottom to top; (2) to trace the events attracting actors, move only downward, descending the lattice. As a convention, the universal upper bound of the lattice contains all the elements in the actor set A, and its universal lower bound contains all the elements in the event set E. Figure 5.5 displays the Galois lattice for the affiliation matrix in Table 5.3. The diagram labels three events as A, B, and C and the five actors as 1, 2, 3, 4, and 5. At the bottom, the lattice contains the largest collection of events. Moving up the lattice encounters an increasingly larger collection of actors but smaller collections of events. The starting point at the bottom has all three events (ABC) but an empty set of actors (ϕ) because no actor attends all events. Moving upward, the lattice graph shows that Events A and B share Actor 1, and Events B and C share Actor 5. Moving farther upward, the subsets of events get smaller but the subsets of actors become larger. Event A attracts Actors 1 and 2, whereas Event B attracts Actors 1, 3, and 5. Event C attracts Actors 4 and 5. The top portion of the lattice lists all actors but no event, indicating that no event attracts all actors in the network. In general, actors that are incident to a line descending from events are affiliated with those events. Actor 1 is incident on lines from Events A and B respectively, indicating that Actor 1 is affiliated with both events. Conversely, events that are incident on the lines ascending from actors attract those actors. For example, Event C is incident on the line ascending from Actor 5, showing that Event C attracts Actor 5. Event B receives lines from both Actors 1 and 5, indicating that both actors attend Event B.

A Galois lattice also shows some affiliation patterns between events and between actors. For example, Figure 5.5 illustrates that Actor 2 does not participate in any other events without Actor 1 (Actor 2 only participates in Event A, with which Actor 1 is also affiliated). Likewise, Actor 4 only participates in Event C, which draws Actor 5. In contrast, neither Actor 1 nor Actor 5 restricts itself in the events that draw Actor 2 or 4, respectively. In other words, the participation in certain event for Actors 1 or 5 is not contingent upon the participation of other actors. From the event's perspective, Figure 5.5 also shows that the three events contain distinctive sets of actors, in the sense that the actors in the three sets are overlapping but not identical. A more elaborated network with more actors and events may reveal some containment structures where certain actors who are present in one event also appear in the other events (Freeman & White, 1993). Thus, the data on all three types of connections can be accurately reconstructed from a Galois lattice—actor-event, actor-actor, and event-event relations.

Despite the clear advantage of using a Galois lattice to examine simultaneously the structural features of all three types of relations, its application is limited to representing only small two-mode network datasets. In this vein, a Galois lattice is similar to a graph, whose principal use is to represent, but not to reduce, data. Large datasets that commonly encompass highly complex structures quickly overwhelm the Galois lattice visualization. Even if reduced symbols are deployed, as proposed by Freeman and White (1993), observers may still experience great difficulty deciphering the images generated by complex Galois lattices.

Galois Lattice of Network Cliques. Analysts suggest that some statistical or algebraic data reduction techniques can be used to simplify the visual representation of a Galois lattice (Duquenne, 1996; White, 1996). Freeman (1996) claimed that Galois lattices could facilitate the representation of cliques among social actors. The classic Luce-Perry definition of a clique presumes a binary symmetric squared matrix (A^2) on a social relation R (Luce & Perry, 1949). A clique C is a maximal subset containing three or more actors among whom all pairs are linked by R. "Maximal" means that no clique can be contained within a larger clique. However, in practice, cliques often are too small, too numerous, or too overlapping to reflect intuitive social group structures (Freeman, 1996, p. 174). The application of Galois lattices to visualize clique structures involves replacing a collection of events with a collection of cliques. We stated before that a Galois lattice is defined with a triple (A, E, I), in which A is a set of actors, E is a set of events, and I is binary relations in $A \times E$. Applying a Galois lattice to cliques, the Galois lattice is redefined with another triple (A, C, and I), in which A and I retain their original meanings, and C indicates a set of cliques.

Following the similar layout as the Galois lattice of events, the Galois lattice of cliques places the larger collection of cliques toward the bottom and the larger collection of actors toward the top. Assuming that Figure 5.5 now shows the Galois lattice of cliques, instead of a lattice of events, at the bottom lies the three cliques ABC with the null set indicating that no actor belongs to all three cliques. Moving up the lattice shows fewer cliques and a larger set of actors. Actor 1 belongs to both Cliques A and B, whereas Actor 5 belongs to both Cliques B and C. Moving further up, Clique A contains Actors 1 and 2, Clique B includes Actors 1, 3, and 5, whereas Clique C has Actors 4 and 5. The entire set of actors lies on the top of the graph, with the null set indicating that no clique encompasses all five actors.

Freeman (1996) discussed several important structural properties in a Galois lattice of network cliques. First, two overlapping cliques will be linked by descending lines that converge at some labeled point lower in the lattice, whereas two nonoverlapping cliques will be linked only at the unlabeled universal lower bound with null set (ϕ). Assuming that Figure 5.5 describes a Galois lattice of network cliques, Cliques A and B converge at a lower point labeled with Actor 1, indicating that the two cliques are overlapping by sharing a common actor, Actor 1. In contrast, Cliques A and C are not overlapping, indicated by their converging point that is at the universal unlabeled lower bound.

Second, Freeman (1996) characterized the position of individual actors in the clique lattice with several key dimensions such as chain, length, height, and depth. A chain is a sequence made up of entirely of ascending lines or entirely of descending lines leading from one element to another. The length of a chain is the number of lines it contains. The height of an actor is the length of chains ascending from the universal lower bound to that actor. In contrast, the depth of an actor is the length of chains from the universal upper bound to that actor. Therefore, actors who appear near the bottom of the lattice would have great depth but low height, whereas actors near the top of the lattice would have great height and low depth. Those actors with great depth but low height are deeply embedded in the network. They participate in several cliques, but their affiliations with those cliques are independent of other actors' affiliations. In one sense, they comprise the core members of the cliques. In contrast, actors with great height but low depth are superficially involved in the network. Their affiliations with certain cliques depend on how others affiliate. Hence, they are the peripheral members of the cliques. Applying those insights to Figure 5.5, we ascertain that Actors 1 and 5 are core members of cliques AB and BC, respectively, whereas Actors 2, 3, and 4 are peripheral to those cliques.

Correspondence Analysis. While lattice analysis represents an algebraic approach to display affiliation networks, *correspondence analysis* uses a scaling technique to achieve a joint display of all the actors and events in an affiliation network (Faust, 2005; Wasserman & Faust, 1994, pp. 291–343). Correspondence analysis is accomplished mainly through a mathematical technique called singular value decomposition (SVD). We have space only to provide a very sketchy description of SVD, focusing on issues directly relevant to affiliation network matrices (for more details, see Strang, 1988).

SVD is a decomposition of matrix $\mathbf{A}$, with dimensions $g \times h$:

$$\mathbf{A} = \mathbf{X} \wedge \mathbf{Y^T} \tag{5.17}$$

The equation contains $\wedge$, which is a diagonal matrix of singular values $\{\lambda_K\}$; $\mathbf{X}$, the matrix of left singular vectors of size $g \times h$; and $\mathbf{Y}$, the matrix of right singular vectors of size $h \times h$. Thus, the left singular vectors refer to the matrix $g \times h$, whereas the right singular vectors refer to the matrix $h \times h$. The number of singular values is also called rank, denoted commonly as W. The SVD uses rank W to scale the actors and events in a graphic display to approximate their entries in $\mathbf{A}$.

The SVD in correspondence analysis involves decomposition of a normalized version of $\mathbf{A}$. Normalization can be produced by two methods: (1) by dividing the entries in original matrix $\mathbf{A}$ by the square root of the product of the row and column marginal totals; or (2) by computing the product of matrix $\mathbf{A}$ times two diagonal matrices, $\mathbf{R}^{-\frac{1}{2}}$ and $\mathbf{C}^{-\frac{1}{2}}$ (Faust, 2005), where

$$\mathbf{R}^{-\frac{1}{2}} = \mathrm{diag}\left(\frac{1}{\sqrt{a_{i+}}}\right) \tag{5.18}$$

$$\mathbf{C}^{-\frac{1}{2}} = \mathrm{diag}\left(\frac{1}{\sqrt{a_{+j}}}\right) \tag{5.19}$$

Multiplying the three matrices produces the normalized version of $\mathbf{A}$, which can also be obtained by dividing the entries in matrix $\mathbf{A}$ by the square root of the product of the row and column marginal totals. Correspondence analysis involves SVD of the resulting product matrix:

$$\mathbf{R}^{-\frac{1}{2}} \mathbf{A} \mathbf{C}^{-\frac{1}{2}} = \mathbf{X} \wedge \mathbf{Y}^T \tag{5.20}$$

Correspondence analysis produces three sets of information: a set of g scores for rows of the matrix, $\mathbf{U} = \{u_{ik}\}$, for $i = 1, 2, \ldots g$ and $k = 1, 2, \ldots w$; a set of h scores for columns of the matrix, $\mathbf{V} = \{v_{jk}\}$, $j = 1, 2, \ldots h$ and $k = 1, 2, \ldots w$; and the singular values $\wedge = \{\lambda_K\}$, for $k = 1, 2, \ldots w$, which indicates the importance of each dimension. To produce a joint display of all the row and column entries, correspondence analysis computes an actor's score as a function of the weighted average event scores with which it is affiliated, and an event's score as a function of the weighted average of its constituent actor scores:

$$\lambda_k u_{ik} = \sum_{j=1}^{h} \frac{\mathbf{a}_{ij}}{\mathbf{a}_{i+}} v_{jk} \qquad (5.21)$$

$$\lambda_k v_{jk} = \sum_{i=1}^{g} \frac{\mathbf{a}_{ij}}{\mathbf{a}_{+j}} u_{ik} \qquad (5.22)$$

In both equations, the $\mathbf{a}_{ij}$ is the entry value of the ith row and the jth column in the original matrix $\mathbf{A}$.

To illustrate, we use our previous example of the affiliation network data consisting of the five actors and three events. Table 5.4 shows the matrix $\mathbf{A}$ in both its original and normalized versions. Table 5.5 shows the SVD of the normalized $\mathbf{A}$, which produces three sets of scores u_{ik}, v_{jk}, and λ_K. Actor scores are a function of the scores of the events with which the actors are affiliated. Likewise, event scores are a function of scores of the actors they attract. In particular, Actor 1's score (-0.661) in the first dimension is derived through the weighted average of the two events with which it is affiliated, divided by the singular value (λ_1): $\frac{\frac{1}{2} \times (-1.146) + \frac{1}{2} \times 0}{0.866} = -0.661$. Likewise, the score for Event 1 in dimension 1 (-1.146) is derived through the weighted average of scores of the actors it attracts (Actors 1 and 2): $\frac{\frac{1}{2} \times (-0.661) + \frac{1}{2} \times (-1.323)}{0.866} = -1.146$. *Can you calculate the scores of other actors and events?*

Figure 5.6 displays the correspondence analysis of the affiliation network. Numbers in parentheses are the scores in both dimensions, identical to their numbers in Table 5.5. The x-axis and y-axis denote the first and second dimensions, respectively (λ). In the diagram, Actor 1, which is affiliated with Events 1 and 2, and Actor 5, affiliated with Events 2 and 3, are central in both dimensions and thus are located at the center of the graph. Event 2 appears at the center of the first dimension, possibly because it attracted the most actors (Actors 1, 3, and 5), but it is slightly farther away from the center of the second dimension than Events 1 and 3, each of which attracted only two actors. Actor 3 is located at the center of the first

TABLE 5.4
Matrix **A** of the Affiliation Network

	e1	*e2*	*e3*
Affiliation Matrix A			
a1	1	1	0
a2	1	0	0
a3	0	1	0
a4	0	0	1
a5	0	1	1
Normalized **A**			
a1	0.5	0.408	0
a2	0.707	0	0
a3	0	0.577	0
a4	0	0	0.707
a5	0	0.408	0.5

TABLE 5.5
Principal Coordinates From the Correspondence
Analysis of the Affiliation Network

Dimensions (w)	*1*	*2*
Actor/Row Scores (u_{ik})		
A1	−0.661	−0.144
A2	−1.323	0.866
A3	0.000	−1.155
A4	1.323	0.866
A5	0.661	−0.144
Event/Column Scores (v_{jk})		
E1	−1.146	0.559
E2	0.000	−0.745
E3	1.146	0.559
Singular Values (λ_k)	0.866	0.645

dimension, due to its affiliation with the central event (Event 2), but Actor 3 also occupies the most peripheral position at the second dimension, possibly because it attended only one event. Actors 2 and 4 are peripheral in both dimensions, reflecting their respective attendance at only one event. Likewise, Events 1 and 3 are also peripheral in both dimensions, suggesting that they attracted fewer participants than did Event 2.

116

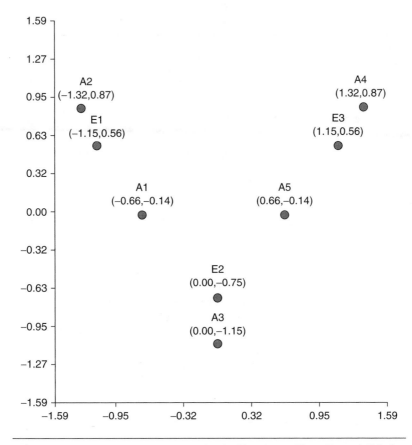

Figure 5.6   Correspondence Analysis of a Five-Actor, Three-Event Affiliation
Network

Conclusion. We discussed several network analysis methods in the preceding paragraphs (cluster analysis, MDS, and correspondence analysis)
that have an important advantage in their applicability to nonnetwork data.
For example, Han (2003) analyzed the 1993 General Social Survey respondents' musical preferences with weighted MDS. Although collecting social
network data can be costly and time-consuming, particularly when using
a complete network design, social survey data are widely available for
creative secondary analyses using those network methods to reveal underlying relationships. Social network analysis gives researchers powerful
conceptual and methodological tools. One recent study skillfully applied

cluster analysis to classify 1,586 civil society Web sites in East Central Europe into six dimensions based on 13 variables (Vedres, Bruszt, & Stark, 2004). Another study (Mohr, 1998) pointedly discussed how to use such methods as MDS, cluster, and correspondence analysis to simplify a complicated structure and to visualize some deep structural logic among different cultural items. Those studies demonstrated the usefulness of familiarity with diverse network methods, which speaks to our ultimate goal for this book—to encourage readers to learn how to decipher structural relations through social network analysis.

REFERENCES

Adamic, L. A., & Adar, E. (2003). Friends and neighbors on the Web. *Social Networks, 25,* 211–230.

Alba, R. D. (1973). A graph-theoretic definition of a sociometric clique. *Journal of Mathematical Sociology, 3,* 113–126.

Aldenderfer, M. S., & Blashfield, R. K. (1984). *Cluster analysis.* Beverly Hills, CA: Sage.

Alderson, A., & Beckfield, J. (2004). Power and position in the world city system. *American Journal of Sociology, 109,* 811–851.

Alexander, M. C., & Danowski, J. (1990). Analysis of an ancient network: Personal communication and the study of social structure in a past society. *Social Networks, 12,* 313–335.

Allison, P. (2001). *Missing data.* Thousand Oaks, CA: Sage.

Anderson, C., Wasserman, S., & Crouch, B. (1999). A p* primer: Logit models for social networks. *Social Networks, 21,* 37–66.

Anderson, J. G., & Jay, S. (1985). Computers and clinical judgement: The role of physician networks. *Social Science and Medicine, 20,* 969–979.

Bailey, S., & Marsden, P. (1999). Interpretation and interview context: Examining the General Social Survey name generator using cognitive methods. *Social Networks, 21,* 287–309.

Baker, W., & Faulkner, R. (1993). The social organization of conspiracy. *American Sociological Review, 58,* 837–860.

Barabási, A.-L. (2002). *Linked: The new science of networks.* Cambridge, MA: Perseus.

Barnes, J. (1954). Class and committees in a Norwegian island parish. *Human Relations, 7,* 39–58.

Barnes, J. A. (1979). Network analysis: Orienting notion, rigorous technique or substantive field of study. In P. W. Holland & S. Leinhardt (Eds.), *Perspectives on social network analysis* (pp. 403–423). New York: Academic Press.

Batchelder, E. (2002). Comparing three simultaneous measurements of a sociocognitive network. *Social Networks, 24,* 261–277.

Bearman, P. S., Moody, J., & Stovel, K. (2004). Chains of affection: The structure of adolescent romantic and sexual networks. *American Journal of Sociology, 110,* 44–91.

Beauchamp, M. (1965). An improved index of centrality. *Behavioral Science, 10,* 161–163.

Benson, M. A. (2004). Dyadic hostility and the ties that bind: State-to-state versus state-to-system security and economic relationships. *Journal of Peace Research, 41,* 659–676.

Berman, F., & Brady, H. (2005). *Final report: NSF SBE-CISE workshop on cyberinfrastructure and the social sciences.* Washington, DC: National Science Foundation.

Bernard, R. H., Johnsen, E., Killworth, P., McCarty, C., Shelley, G., & Robinson, S. (1990). Comparing four different methods for measuring personal social networks. *Social Networks, 12,* 179–215.

Bernard, R. H., & Killworth, P. (1977). Informant accuracy in social network data II. *Human Communications Research, 4,* 3–18.

Bernard, R. H., Killworth, P., & Sailer, L. (1981). Summary of research on informant accuracy in network data, and on the reverse small world problem. *Connections, 4*(2), 11–25.

Bernard, R. H., Killworth, P., Sailer, L., & Kronenfeld, D. (1984). The problem of informant accuracy: The validity of retrospective data. *Annual Review of Anthropology, 13,* 495–517.

Blau, P. M., Ruan, D., & Ardelt, M. (1991). Interpersonal choice and networks in China. *Social Forces, 69,* 1037–1062.

Boorman, S., & White, H. (1976). Social structure from multiple networks. II. Role structures. *American Journal of Sociology, 81,* 1384–1446.

Borgatti, S., & Everett, M. (1992). Notions of position in social network analysis. *Sociological Methodology, 22,* 1–35.

Borgatti, S., Everett, M., & Freeman, L. (2004). *UCINET VI software for social network analysis.* Natick, MA: Analytic Technologies.

Borgatti, S., Everett, M., & Shirey, P. (1990). LS sets, lambda sets and other cohesive subsets. *Social Networks, 12,* 337–357.

Borgatti, S., & Molina, J.-L. (2005). Towards ethical guidelines for network research in organizations. *Social Networks, 27,* 107–117.

Borgatti, S. P. (2003). The key player problem. In R. Breiger, K. Carley, & P. Pattison (Eds.), *Dynamic social network modeling and analysis: Workshop summary and papers* (pp. 241–252). Washington, DC: National Academy of Sciences Press.

Brandes, U., Kenis, P., Raab, J., Schneider, V., & Wagner, D. (1999). Explorations into the visualization of policy networks. *Journal of Theoretical Politics, 11,* 75–106.

Brewer, D. D. (2000). Forgetting in the recall-based elicitation of personal and social networks. *Social Networks, 22,* 29–43.

Brewer, D. D., & Webster, C. (1999). Forgetting of friends and its effects on measuring friendship networks. *Social Networks, 21,* 361–373.

Burgin, R. (1995). The retrieval effectiveness of five clustering algorithms as a function of indexing exhaustivity. *Journal of the American Society for Information Science, 46*(8), 562–572.

Burt, R. (1983). Range. In R. S. Burt & M. Minor (Eds.), *Applied network analysis: A methodological introduction.* Beverly Hills, CA: Sage.

Burt, R. (1985). General social survey network items. *Connections, 8,* 119–123.

Burt, R. (1987). A note on missing network data in the General Social Survey. *Social Networks, 9,* 63–73.

Burt, R. S. (1978). Cohesion versus structural equivalence as a basis for network subgroups. *Sociological Methods and Research, 7,* 189–212.

Burt, R. S. (1979). Disaggregating the effect on profits in manufacturing industries of having imperfectly competitive consumers and suppliers. *Social Science Research, 8*(2), 120–143.

Burt, R. S. (1983). Distinguishing relational contents. In R. S. Burt & M. J. Minor (Eds.), *Applied network analysis* (pp. 35–74). Beverly Hills, CA: Sage.

Burt, R. S. (1992). *Structural holes: The social structure of competition.* Cambridge, MA: Harvard University Press.

Campbell, K. E., & Lee, B. (1991). Name generators in surveys of personal networks. *Social Networks, 13,* 203–221.

Campbell, K. E., Marsden, P., & Hurlbert, J. (1986). Social resources and socioeconomic status. *Social Networks, 8,* 97–117.

Carley, K., & Krackhardt, D. (1996). Cognitive inconsistencies and non-symmetric friendship. *Social Networks, 18,* 1–27.

Carrington, P., Scott, J., & Wasserman, S. (Eds.). (2005). *Models and methods in social network analysis.* New York: Cambridge University Press.

Casciaro, T. (1998). Seeing things clearly: Social structure, personality, and accuracy in social network perception. *Social Networks, 20,* 331–351.

Cohen, S., Frank, E., Doyle, W. J., Skoner, D. P., Rabin, B. S., & Gwaltney, J. M., Jr. (1998). Types of stressors that increase susceptibility to the common cold in adults. *Health Psychology, 17,* 214–223.

Coleman, J. S. (1986). Social theory, social research, and a theory of action. *American Journal of Sociology, 91,* 1309–1335.

Cowan, R., & Jonard, N. (2004). Network structure and the diffusion of knowledge. *Journal of Economic Dynamics and Control, 28,* 1557–1575.

Cross, R., Liedtka, J., & Weiss, L. (2005). A practical guide to social networks. *Harvard Business Review, 83*(3), 124–132.

Crouch, B., & Wasserman, S. (1998). A practical guide to fitting social network models via logistic regression. *Connections, 21,* 87–101.

Davis, J. A. (1979). The Davis/Holland/Leinhardt studies: An overview. In P. W. Holland & S. Leinhardt (Eds.), *Perspectives on social network research* (pp. 51–62). New York: Academic Press.

Degenne, A., & Forse, M. (1999). *Introducing social networks.* Thousand Oaks, CA: Sage.

Diani, M., & McAdam, D. (Eds.). (2003). *Social movements and networks: Relational approaches to collective action.* New York: Oxford University Press.

Doreian, P., Batagelj, V., & Ferligoj, A. (2005). *Generalized blockmodeling.* Cambridge, UK: Cambridge University Press.

Doreian, P., & Woodard, K. (1992). Fixed list versus snowball selection of social networks. *Social Science Research, 21,* 216–233.

Doreian, P., & Woodard, K. (1994). Defining and locating cores and boundaries of social networks. *Social Networks, 16,* 267–293.

Dunbar, R. I. M., & Spoor, M. (1995). Social networks, support cliques and kinship. *Human Nature, 6,* 273–290.

Duquenne, V. (1996). On lattice approximations: Syntactic aspects. *Social Networks, 18,* 189–199.

Emirbayer, M. (1997). Manifesto for a relational sociology. *American Journal of Sociology, 103,* 281–317.

Erickson, B. H. (1996). Culture, class, and connections. *American Journal of Sociology, 102,* 217–251.

Erickson, B. H. (2004). The distribution of gendered social capital in Canada. In H. Flap & B. Volker (Eds.), *Creation and returns of social capital: A new research program* (pp. 27–51). New York: Routledge.

Everett, M. (1985). Role similarity and complexity in social networks. *Social Networks, 7,* 353–359.

Everett, M., Boyd, J., & Borgatti, S. (1990). Ego-centered and local roles: A graph theoretic approach. *Journal of Mathematical Sociology, 15,* 163–172.

Fafchamps, M., van der Leij, M. J., & Goyal, S. (2006). *Scientific networks and co-authorship (No. 256).* University of Oxford, Department of Economics, Economics Series Working Papers.

Faust, K. (1988). Comparison of methods for positional analysis: Structural and general equivalences. *Social Networks, 10,* 313–341.

Faust, K. (1997). Centrality in affiliation networks. *Social Networks, 19,* 157–191.

Faust, K. (2005). Using correspondence analysis for joint displays of affiliation networks. In P. J. Carrington, J. Scott, & S. Wasserman (Eds.), *Models and methods in social network analysis* (pp. 117–147). New York: Cambridge University Press.

Faust, K., & Skvoretz, J. (2002). Comparing networks across space and time, size and species. *Sociological Methodology, 32,* 267–299.

Feld, S. L., & Carter, W. C. (2002). Detecting measurement bias in respondent reports of personal networks. *Social Networks, 24,* 365–383.

Feldman-Savelsberg, P., Ndonko, F. L., & Yang, S. (2005). How rumor begets rumor: Collective memory, ethnic conflict, and reproductive rumors in Cameroon. In G. A. Fine, V. Campion-Vincent, & C. Heath (Eds.), *Rumor mills: The social impact of rumor and legend* (pp. 141–159). New York: Transaction Press.

Fischer, C. S. (1982). What do we mean by "friend"? An inductive study. *Social Networks, 3,* 287–306.

Fischer, C. S., & Shavit, Y. (1995). National differences in network density: Israel and the United States. *Social Networks, 17,* 129–145.

Frank, O. (2003). *KliqFinder for Windows, version 0.05.* East Lansing: Michigan State University.

Frank, O. (2005). Network sampling and model fitting. In P. Carrington, J. Scott, & S. Wasserman (Eds.), *Models and methods in social network analysis* (pp. 31–45). New York: Cambridge University Press.

Frank, O., & Snijders, T. A. B. (1994). Estimating the size of hidden populations using snowball sampling. *Journal of Official Statistics, 10,* 53–67.

Frank, O., & Strauss, D. (1986). Markov graphs. *Journal of the American Statistical Association, 81,* 832–842.

Freeman, L. (1977). A set of measures of centrality based upon betweenness. *Sociometry, 40,* 35–41.

Freeman, L. (1979). Centrality in social networks: I. Conceptual clarification. *Social Networks, 1,* 215–239.

Freeman, L. C. (1992). Filling in the blanks: A theory of cognitive categories and the structure of social affiliation. *Social Psychology Quarterly, 55,* 118–127.

Freeman, L. C. (1992). The resurrection of cliques: Application of Galois lattices. *Bulletin de Methodologie Sociologique, 37,* 3–24.

Freeman, L. C. (1996). Some antecedents of social network analysis. *Connections, 19,* 39–42.

Freeman, L. C. (2000). Visualizing social networks. *Journal of Social Structure, 1,* 1–15.

Freeman, L. C. (2004). *The development of social network analysis: A study in the sociology of science.* Vancouver, Canada: Empirical Press.

Freeman, L. C. (2005). Graphic techniques for exploring social network data. In P. J. Carrington, J. Scott, & S. Wasserman (Eds.), *Models and methods in social network analysis* (pp. 248–270). Cambridge, MA: Cambridge University Press.

Freeman, L. C., Borgatti, S., & White, D. (1991). Centrality in valued graphs: A measure of betweenness based on network flow. *Social Networks, 13,* 141–154.

Freeman, L. C., Romney, K., & Freeman, S. (1987). Cognitive structure and informant accuracy. *American Anthropologist, 89*(2), 310–325.

Freeman, L. C., & Thompson, C. R. (1989). Estimating acquaintanceship volume. In M. Kochen (Ed.), *The small world* (pp. 147–158). Norwood, NJ: Ablex.

Freeman, L. C., & Webster, C. (1994). Interpersonal proximity in social and cognitive space. *Social Cognition, 12*(3), 223–247.

Freeman, L. C., & White, D. (1993). Using Galois lattices to represent network data. *Sociological Methodology, 23,* 127–146.

Galaskiewicz, J. (1979). The structure of community organizational networks. *Social Forces, 57,* 1346–1364.

Goodman, L. (1961). Snowball sampling. *The Annals of Mathematical Statistics, 32,* 148–170.

Granovetter, M. (1973). The strength of weak ties. *American Journal of Sociology, 78,* 1360–1380.

Han, S. (2003). Unraveling the brow: What and how of choice in musical preference. *Sociological Perspectives, 46,* 435–459.

Harary, F. (1969). *Graph theory.* Reading, MA: Addison-Wesley.

Hargens, L. L. (2000). Using the literature: Reference networks, reference contexts, and the social structure of scholarship. *American Sociological Review, 65,* 846–865.

Harrisson, D., Laplante, N., & St-Cyr, L. (2001). Cooperation and resistance in work innovation networks. *Human Relations, 54,* 215–255.

Heckathorn, D. (1997). Respondent-driven sampling: A new approach to the study of hidden populations. *Social Problems, 44,* 174–199.

Heider, F. (1958). *The psychology of interpersonal relations.* New York: Wiley.

Holland, P. W., & Leinhardt, S. (1981). An exponential family of probability distributions for directed graphs. *Journal of the American Statistical Association, 76,* 33–65.

Huisman, M., & van Duijn, M. A. J. (2005). Software for social network analysis. In P. J. Carrington, J. Scott, & S. Wasserman (Eds.), *Models and methods in social network analysis* (pp. 270–316). New York: Cambridge University Press.

Johnson, J., & Orbach, M. (2002). Perceiving the political landscape: Ego biases in cognitive political networks. *Social Networks, 24,* 291–310.

Jolly, A. M., Muth, S. Q., Wylie, J. L., & Potterat, J. J. (2001). Sexual networks and sexually transmitted infections: A tale of two cities. *Journal of Urban Health, 78*(3), 433–445.

Jones, L. M., & Fischer, C. S. (1978). *Studying egocentric network by mass survey.* Working Paper at the Institute of Urban and Regional Development, University of California, Berkeley.

Kang, S.-Y., Deren, S., Andia, J., Colon, H. M., & Robles, R. (2005). Egocentric HIV risk networks among Puerto Rican crack users in New York and in Puerto Rico: Impact on sex risk behaviors over time. *AIDS Education and Prevention, 17,* 53–67.

Kenis, P., & Knoke, D. (2002). How organizational field networks shape interorganizational tie-formation rates. *Academy of Management Review, 27,* 275–293.

Killworth, P., Johnsen, E., Bernard, R., Shelley, G., & McCarty, C. (1990). Estimating the size of personal networks. *Social Networks, 12,* 289–312.

Killworth, P. D., Bernard, R., & McCarty, C. (1984). Measuring patterns of acquaintanceship. *Current Anthropology, 25,* 381–392.

Kirke, D. M. (1996). Collecting peer data and delineating peer networks in a complete network. *Social Networks, 18,* 333–346.

Klovdahl, A. S. (2005). Social network research and human subjects protection: Towards more effective infectious disease control. *Social Networks, 27,* 119–137.

Knoke, D. (2001). *Changing organizations: Business networks in the new political economy.* Boulder, CO: Westview Press.

Knoke, D. (in press). Playing well together: Creating corporate social capital in strategic alliance networks. *American Behavioral Scientist.*

Knoke, D., & Burt, R. (1983). Prominence. In R. S. Burt & M. J. Miner (Eds.), *Applied network analysis: A methodological introduction* (pp. 195–222). Beverly Hills CA: Sage.

Knoke, D., & Kuklinski, J. H. (1982). *Network analysis.* Beverly Hills, CA: Sage.

Knoke, D., & Laumann, E. O. (1982). The social structure of national policy domains: An exploration of some structural hypotheses. In P. V. Marsden & N. Lin (Eds.), *Social structure and network analysis* (pp. 255–270). Beverly Hills, CA: Sage.

Knoke, D., Pappi, F. U., Broadbent, J., & Tsujinaka, Y. (1996). *Comparing policy networks: Labor politics in the U.S., Germany, and Japan.* New York: Cambridge University Press.

Knoke, D., & Rogers, D. (1979). A blockmodel analysis of interorganizational networks. *Sociology and Social Research, 64,* 28–52.

Knox, H., Savage, M., & Harvey, P. (2006). Social networks and the study of relations: Networks as method, metaphor and form. *Economy and Society, 35,* 113–140.

Koehly, L. M., & Pattison, P. (2005). Random graph models for social networks: Multiple relations or multiple raters. In P. J. Carrington, J. Scott, & S. Wasserman (Eds.), *Models and methods in social network analysis* (pp. 162–191). New York: Cambridge University Press.

Kossinets, G. (2003). Effects of missing data in social networks. *Social Networks, 28,* 247–268.

Krackhardt, D. (1987). Cognitive social structures. *Social Networks, 9,* 109–134.

Krackhardt, D., & Kilduff, M. (1999). Whether close or far: Perceptions of balance in friendship networks in organizations. *Journal of Personality and Social Psychology, 76,* 770–782.

Kronenfeld, D. B., & Kronenfeld, J. (1972). Toward a science of design for successful food service. *Institutions and Volume Feeding Management, 70,* 38–44.

Kruskal, J. B., & Wish, M. (1978). *Multidimensional scaling.* Beverly Hills, CA: Sage.

Kumbasar, E., Romney, K., & Batchelder, W. (1994). Systematic biases in social perception. *American Journal of Sociology, 100,* 477–505.

LaPierre, R. T. (1934). Attitudes vs. actions. *Social Forces, 13,* 230–237.

Laumann, E., Marsden, P. V., & Prensky, D. (1983). The boundary-specification problem in network analysis. In R. Burt & M. Minor (Eds.), *Applied network analysis* (pp. 18–34). Beverly Hills, CA: Sage.

Laumann, E. O., & Knoke, D. (1987). *The organizational state: Social choice in national policy domains.* Madison: University of Wisconsin Press.

Laumann, E. O., Mardsen, P. V., & Prensky, D. (1989). The boundary specification problem in network analysis. In L. C. Freeman, D. R. White, & A. K. Romney (Eds.), *Research methods in social network analysis* (pp. 61–87). Fairfax, VA: George Mason University Press.

Lin, N. (1982). Social resources and instrumental action. In P. V. Marsden & N. Lin (Eds.), *Social structure and network analysis* (pp. 131–145). Beverly Hills, CA: Sage.

Lin, N., & Dumin, M. (1986). Access to occupations through social ties. *Social Networks, 8,* 365–385.

Lin, N., Fu, Y., & Hsung, R.-M. (2001). The position generator: Measurement techniques for investigations of social capital. In N. Lin, K. Cook, & R. Burt (Eds.), *Social capital: Theory and research* (pp. 57–81). Hawthorne, NY: Aldine de Gruyter.

Luce, D., & Perry, A. D. (1949). A method of matrix analysis of group structure. *Psychometrika, 14,* 95–116.

Marsden, P. (2002). Egocentric and sociocentric measures of network centrality. *Social Networks, 24,* 407–422.

Marsden, P. V. (1987). Core discussion networks of Americans. *American Sociological Review, 52,* 122–131.

Marsden, P. V. (1993). The reliability of network density and composition measures. *Social Networks, 15*(4), 399–421.

Marsden, P. V. (2005). Recent developments in network measurement. In P. Carrington, J. Scott, & S. Wasserman, *Models and methods in social network analysis* (pp. 8–30). New York: Cambridge University Press.

McCarty, C., Bernard, R., Killworth, P., Shelley, G., & Johnsen, E. (1997). Eliciting representative samples of personal networks. *Social Networks, 19,* 303–323.

McPherson, M., Smith-Lovin, L., & Brashears, M. E. (2006). Social isolation in America: Changes in core discussion networks over two decades. *American Sociological Review, 71,* 353–375.

Meyer, M. (2000). What is special about patent citations? Differences between scientific and patent citations. *Scientometrics, 49*(1), 93–123.

Mische, A., & Pattison, P. E. (2000). Composing a civic arena: Publics, projects, and social settings. *Poetics, 27,* 163–194.

Mitchell, J. C. (1969). *Social networks in urban situations: Analyses of personal relationships in Central African towns.* Manchester, UK: Manchester University Press.

Mohr, J. W. (1998). Measuring meaning structures. *Annual Review of Sociology, 24,* 345–370.

Mohr, J. W., & Duquenne, V. (1997). The duality of culture and practice: Poverty relief in New York City, 1888–1917. *Theory and Society, 26,* 305–356.

124

Mokken, R. J. (1979). Cliques, clubs and clans. *Quantity and Quality, 13,* 161–173.

Moreno, J. L. (1934). *Who shall survive?* Washington, DC: Nervous and Mental Disease Publishing Company.

Morrissey, J., Tausig, M., & Lindsey, M. (1985). *Network analytic methods for mental health service system research: A comparison of two community support systems (No. 6).* Washington, DC: National Institute of Mental Health Series BN.

Mouttapa, M., Valente, T. W., & Gallaher, P. (2004). Social network predictors of bullying and victimization. *Adolescence, 39,* 315–335.

Nadel, S. F. (1957). *The theory of social structure.* London: Cohen and West.

Neuman, W. L. (2000). *Social research methods: Qualitative and quantitative approaches* (4th ed.). Boston: Allyn & Bacon.

Newcomb, T. (1961). *The acquaintance process.* New York: Holt, Rinehart and Winston.

Newman, M. E. J. (2003). The structure and function of complex networks. *SIAM Review, 45,* 167–256.

de Nooy, W., Mrvar, W. A., & Batagelj, V. (2005). *Exploratory social network analysis with Pajek.* New York: Cambridge University Press.

Nowicki, K., & Snijders, T. (2001). Estimation and prediction for stochastic blockstructures. *Journal of the American Statistical Association, 96*(455), 1077–1088.

Nyblom, J., Borgatti, S., Roslakka, J., & Salo, M. A. (2003). Statistical analysis of network data: An application to diffusion of innovation. *Social Networks, 25,* 175–195.

Padgett, J. F., & Ansell, C. K. (1993). Robust action and the rise of the Medici, 1400–1434. *American Journal of Sociology, 98,* 1259–1319.

Pampel , F. C. (2000). *Logistic regression: A primer.* Thousand Oaks, CA: Sage.

Pattison, P. (1988). Network models: Some comments on papers in this special issue. *Social Networks, 10,* 383–411.

Pattison, P., & Wasserman, S. (1999). Logit models and logistic regressions for social networks: II. Multivariate relations. *British Journal of Mathematical and Statistical Psychology, 52,* 169–193.

Peay, E. R. (1980). Connectedness in a general model for valued networks. *Social Networks, 2,* 385–410.

Perrow, C. (1986). *Complex organizations: A critical essay.* New York: Random House.

Podolny, J. M., & Stuart, T. (1995). A role-based ecology of technological change. *American Journal of Sociology, 100,* 1224–1260.

Raab, J., & Milward, H. B. (2003). Dark networks as problems. *Journal of Public Administration Research and Theory, 13,* 413–439.

Rice, R. (1990). Computer-mediated communication system network data: Theoretical concerns and empirical examples. *International Journal of Man-Machine Studies, 32,* 627–647.

Rice, R. (1994). Network analysis and computer-mediated communication systems. In S. Wasserman & J. Galaskiewicz (Eds.), *Advances in social network analysis* (pp. 167–203). Newbury Park, CA: Sage.

Rice, R., Borgman, C., Bednarski, D., & Hart, P. J. (1989). Journal-to-journal citation data: Issues of reliability and validity. *Scientometrics, 15,* 257–282.

Robins, G., Pattison, P., & Wasserman, S. (1999). Logit models and logistic regressions for social networks: III. Valued relations. *Psychometrika, 64,* 371–394.

Romney, K., & Weller, S. (1984). Predicting informant accuracy from patterns of recall among individuals. *Social Networks, 6,* 59–77.

Romney, K., Weller, S., & Batchelder, W. (1986). Culture as consensus: A theory of culture and informant accuracy. *American Anthropologist, 88,* 313–338.

Ruan, D. (1998). The content of the General Social Survey discussion networks: An exploration of General Social Survey discussion name generator in a Chinese context. *Social Networks, 20,* 247–264.

Ruan, D., Freeman, L., Dai, X., Pan, Y., & Zhang, W. (1997). On the changing structure of social networks in urban China. *Social Networks, 19,* 75–89.

Sabidussi, G. (1966). The centrality index of a graph. *Psychometrika, 31,* 581–603.

Salganik, M. J., & Heckathorn, D. D. (2004). Sampling and estimation in hidden populations using respondent-driven sampling. *Sociological Methodology, 34,* 193–240.

Schiffman, S., Reynolds, L., & Young, F. (1981). *Introduction to multidimensional scaling.* New York: Academic Press.

Schwartz, J. E. (1977). An examination of CONCOR and related methods for blocking sociometric data. *Sociological Methodology, 7,* 255–282.

Schweizer, T. (1996). Actor and event orderings across time: Lattice representation and Boolean analysis of political disputes in Chen Village, China. *Social Networks, 18,* 247–266.

Scott, J. (1991). *Social network analysis: A handbook.* London: Sage.

Scott, J. (2000). *Social network analysis: A handbook* (2nd ed.). Thousand Oaks, CA: Sage.

Seidman, S. B. (1983). Network structure and minimum degree. *Social Networks, 5,* 269–287.

Simmel, G. (1908). *Sociology: Investigations on the forms of sociation.* Leipzig, Germany: Duncker and Humblot.

Slez, A., & Martin, J. L. (2007). Political action and party formation in the United States constitutional convention. *American Sociological Review, 72*(1), 42–67.

Smith, D., & Timberlake, M. (2002). Hierarchies of dominance among world cities: A network approach. In S. Sassen (Ed.), *Global networks, linked cities* (pp. 117–141). New York: Routledge.

Snijders, T. A. B., Steglich, C., Schweinberger, M., & Huisman, M. (2007). *Manual for SIENA version 3.* Groningen, Netherlands: University of Groningen, ICS, Department of Sociology.

Stoebenau, K., & Valente, T. W. (2003). Using network analysis to understand community-based programs: A case study from highland Madagascar. *International Family Planning Perspectives, 29*(4), 167–173.

Stork, D., & Richards, W. (1992). Nonrespondents in communication network studies: Problems and possibilities. *Group & Organization Management, 17*(2), 193–210.

Strang, G. (1988). *Linear algebra and its applications* (3rd ed.). San Diego: Harcourt, Brace, Jovanovich.

Strauss, D., & Ikeda, M. (1990). Pseudolikelihood estimation for social networks. *Journal of the American Statistical Association, 85,* 204–212.

Taylor, S., & Fiske, S. (1978). Salience, attention, and attribution: Top-of-the-head phenomena. In L. Berkowitz (Ed.), *Advances in experimental social psychology, (vol. 11)* pp. 249–288. New York: Academic Press.

Tenkasi, R. V., & Chesmore, M. C. (2003). Social networks and planned organizational change: The impact of strong network ties on effective change implementation and use. *Journal of Applied Behavioral Science, 39,* 281–300.

Tsuji, R. (1997). *PermNet, version 0.94.* Sapporo: Hokkaido University.

Tsvetovat, M., & Carley, K. M. (2005). Structural knowledge and success of anti-terrorist activity: The downside of structural equivalence [Electronic version]. *Journal of Social Structure, 6*(2).

Useem, M. (1979). The social organization of the American business elite and participation of corporation directors in the governance of American institutions. *American Sociological Review, 44,* 553–572.

Valente, T. (1995). *Network models of the diffusion of innovations*. Cresskill, NJ: Hampton Press.

Van der Gaag, M., & Snijders, T. (2004). Proposals for the measurement of individual social capital. In H. Flap & B. Volker (Eds.), *Creation and returns of social capital: A new research program* (pp. 199–219). New York: Routledge.

Vedres, B., Bruszt, L., & Stark, D. (2004). Organizing technologies: Genre forms of online civic association in Eastern Europe. *Annals of the American Academy of Political and Social Science, 597,* 171–188.

Wasserman, S., & Faust, K. (1994). *Social network analysis: Methods and applications*. New York: Cambridge University Press.

Wasserman, S., & Pattison, P. (1996). Logit models and logistic regressions for social networks: I. An introduction to Markov graphs and p. *Psychometrika, 61*(3), 401–425.

Wasserman, S., & Robins, G. (2005). An introduction to random graphs, dependence graphs, and p*. In P. J. Carrington, J. Scott, & S. Wasserman (Eds.), *Models and methods in social network analysis* (pp. 148–161). New York: Cambridge University Press.

Watts, D. J. (2003). *Six degrees: The science of a connected age*. New York: Norton.

Wellman, B. (1999). From little boxes to loosely bounded networks: The privatization and domestication of community. In J. L. Abu-Lughod (Ed.), *Sociology for the twenty-first century* (pp. 94–114). Chicago: University of Chicago Press.

Wellman, B., & Berkowitz, S. D. (1988). *Social structures: A network approach*. Cambridge, UK: Cambridge University Press.

White, D. (1996). Statistical entailments and the Galois lattice. *Social Networks, 18,* 201–215.

White, D., & Reitz, K. (1983). Graph and semigroup homomorphisms on networks of relations. *Social Networks, 5,* 193–234.

White, H. C., Boorman, S. A., & Breiger, R. L. (1976). Social structure from multiple networks, I: Blockmodels of roles and positions. *American Journal of Sociology, 81,* 730–780.

White, K., & Watkins, S. C. (2000). Accuracy, stability and reciprocity in informal conversational networks in rural Kenya. *Social Networks, 22,* 337–355.

White, M., Kim, A., & Glick, J. J. (2005). Mapping social segregation. *Sociological Methods and Research, 34,* 173–203.

Winship, C., & Mandel, M. (1983). Roles and positions: A critique and extension of the block-modeling approach. *Sociological Methodology, 14,* 314–344.

Wu, L. L. (1983). Local blockmodel algebras for analyzing social networks. *Sociological Methodology, 14,* 272–313.

Yang, S., & Hexmoor, H. (2004). Measuring optimal connections in large networks: A new algorithm and its application. *Journal of Mathematical Sociology, 28*(3), 197–213.

Yang, S., & Knoke, D. (2001). Optimal connections: Strengths and distance in valued graphs. *Social Networks, 23,* 285–295.

INDEX

ABOUT THE AUTHORS

David Knoke (Ph.D., University of Michigan, 1972) coauthored *Network Analysis* (1982) and has published 15 books and more than a hundred articles and book chapters, primarily on organizations, networks, politics, and social statistics. He was principal coinvestigator on several National Science Foundation–funded projects on voluntary associations, lobbying organizations in national policy domains, and organizational surveys of diverse establishments. A current project on the Global Information Sector examines strategic alliance network evolution among international corporations. At the University of Minnesota, Twin Cities, he teaches a graduate social network analysis seminar that attracts students from diverse disciplines. He appreciates support from the College of Liberal Arts Faculty Sabbatical Supplement Program during a portion of this book's preparation.

Song Yang (Ph.D., University of Minnesota, 2002) authored *Investigating Job Training Programs in U.S. Organizations* (2003) and has published 15 articles and book chapters on issues related to work and workplaces, and social network analysis. He is working on several proposals to study various human resources policies and programs in Chinese organizations, focusing on emergent stratification structures and underpinning factors behind those stratification. He teaches methodology and statistics to both graduate and undergraduate students at the University of Arkansas.